Augustus Samuel Wilkins

**National Education in Greece in the Fourth Century before Christ**

Augustus Samuel Wilkins

**National Education in Greece in the Fourth Century before Christ**

ISBN/EAN: 9783337165116

Hergestellt in Europa, USA, Kanada, Australien, Japan

Cover: Foto ©ninafisch / pixelio.de

Weitere Bücher finden Sie auf **www.hansebooks.com**

# NATIONAL EDUCATION
IN GREECE

PREPARING FOR PUBLICATION.

A NEW

## SERIES OF LATIN CLASS-BOOKS,

FOR USE IN SCHOOLS 'AND COLLEGES,

Conducted by AUGUSTUS S. WILKINS, M.A., Fellow of University College, London; Professor of Latin in the Owens College, Manchester; and Assistant Examiner in the University of London.

*Arrangements have been made for the early publication of the following volumes:—*

1. A LATIN GRAMMAR, by AUGUSTUS S. WILKINS, M.A.

2. A FIRST LATIN BOOK, by F. W. HASLAM, M.A., Composition Master in the Tunbridge Grammar School.

3. A FIRST LATIN READING BOOK, by E. B. ENGLAND, M.A., Assistant Lecturer in Classics in the Owens College, Manchester.

4. EXERCISES IN LATIN SYNTAX, by A. G. SYMONDS, M.A., Lecturer in Composition to the Owens College Evening Classes.

5. CICERO DE AMICITIA, with Notes and Excursus, by the Rev. R. DIXON, M.A., Head Master of the Nottingham High School.

*₊* The Series will be continued without intermission, and will include Annotated Texts of the principal Authors read in Schools and Colleges.

LONDON: STRAHAN & Co.

### In the Fourth Century before Christ

By AUGUSTUS S. WILKINS, M.A.,

FELLOW OF UNIVERSITY COLLEGE, LONDON;
LATE SCHOLAR OF ST. JOHN'S COLLEGE, CAMBRIDGE;
PROFESSOR OF LATIN IN THE OWENS COLLEGE, MANCHESTER

STRAHAN & CO.
56, LUDGATE HILL, LONDON.
1873

LONDON:
PRINTED BY VIRTUE AND CO.,
CITY ROAD.

TO THE RIGHT REVEREND
## CONNOP THIRLWALL, D.D.,
LORD BISHOP OF ST. DAVID'S,

I Dedicate,

WITH PROFOUND VENERATION,

AN ESSAY,

WHOSE ONLY CLAIM ON THE NOTICE OF THE FIRST

OF LIVING ENGLISH HISTORIANS IS,

THAT IT COMES ASSOCIATED, HOWEVER UNWORTHILY,

WITH THE NAME OF

JULIUS CHARLES HARE.

# PREFACE.

THE following essay obtained the Hare Prize in the University of Cambridge, a prize founded in 1861 by the friends of the Ven. Archdeacon Hare, "to testify their admiration for his character, and the high sense they entertained of his services to learning and religion." It is awarded once in every four years to the graduate of not more than ten years' standing from his first degree, who shall produce the best English Dissertation on some subject taken from Ancient Greek or Roman History, political or literary, or from the History of Greek or Roman Philosophy. The subject proposed by the Vice-Chancellor for the year 1873 was "The Theories and Practice of

National Education in Greece during the Fourth Century B.C."

The subject of Greek education has been so thoroughly investigated, the passages in classical authors that bear upon it have been so industriously collected, and its principal merits and defects have been so fully expounded, that it is difficult now to write upon it with any originality. In this essay my aim has been mainly twofold, to group the facts familiar to every scholar round the idea of the relation of the State to the citizen, and to furnish a trustworthy sketch of this side of the life and thought of Greece for the use of the general reader. Now that the supreme importance of national education is happily so widely recognised, there are probably many who, though not having the power of studying for themselves the classical authors, still desire to know how the problems which are straining so severely the statesmen of to-day, were solved in the ancient world. I do not know any work in English which exactly suits this want, and therefore I have endeavoured to adapt this essay to the needs of a wider circle than that to which, under other circumstances, it might have seemed fitter to appeal. The authorities used are in all cases referred to in the margin. In dealing with Plato, I have been deeply indebted to his two great English exponents and critics. In other cases I have drawn chiefly on the scholars of Germany; but all references to classical authors have been independently examined and verified. Unfortunately, the admirable sketch of the history of education among the Greeks and Romans by the well-known Danish scholar, J. L. Ussing (translated into German by Friedrichsen. Altona, 1870), and the copious collection of materials by K. F. Hermann in his Privatalterthümer (2nd edition by Stark. Heidelberg, 1870), did not reach me until I had written these pages. References to them have here and there been added in the course of revision

# CONTENTS.

### CHAPTER I.
INTRODUCTORY—EDUCATION IN SPARTA . . 1

### CHAPTER II.
EDUCATION AT ATHENS . . . . . . 60

### CHAPTER III.
PLATO ON EDUCATION . . . . . . 101

### CHAPTER IV.
ARISTOTLE ON EDUCATION . . . . . 135

# CHAPTER I.

## INTRODUCTORY.—NATIONAL EDUCATION IN SPARTA.

THE object of the present essay will be to set forth, so far as our extant authorities allow—1st, the popular Greek conceptions of the aims and methods of national education; 2nd, the manner in which these conceptions were carried into practical effect, with their general results upon national life; and 3rd, the criticisms of the popular ideas and methods of education passed by the great Greek thinkers of the fourth century before our era, with the substitutes suggested by them. *Object of the essay.*

In attempting to deal with these questions successively our attention will of necessity be limited almost wholly to *Limits of the inquiry.*

Athens and Sparta. It is true that for a portion of the century under our more immediate consideration the hegemony of Greece falls to the lot of Thebes. But her supremacy was too brief and baseless for the thought of the Athenian writers (on whom we have mainly to depend) to be attracted to her institutions, social or political, in the same way in which it was challenged by those of Lacedaemon. The Theban views and methods of education will therefore claim our notice rather by way of occasional contrast and comparison than as an independent portion of our inquiries. And in regard to the other Hellenic communities, we find in almost every case, either that we have but hints and fragments of information which whet our interest rather than satisfy it, or that our authorities treat of periods excluded from this essay by the limits of time imposed. Magna Graecia, the Aeolic colonies of Lesbos and the adjacent coast, Crete and Ionia, would all furnish matter of value for a general history of Greek education, which must here be regarded as excluded.

But happily the states on which we have *Athens and Sparta typical states.* the fullest information are not only those of the greatest intrinsic interest, but they may also be regarded as typical. From the earliest appearance of the Hellenic race on the stage of history, it presents itself to us as broadly divided into two great sections.* The division was never deep enough to sever the bond which united all together as members of a common Hellas; nor did it exclude numerous and occasionally important sub-divisions. Still, speaking with a certain latitude, we may say that a careful study of the leading characteristics of the Dorian and Ionian races, and their mutual influence, will give us almost all we want for a knowledge of the mental and spiritual life of Hellas.† Now of these two races, Athens and Sparta were undoubtedly the recognised leaders and representatives; and therefore, if we

---

\* E. Curtius has well shown that minor divisions sink into insignificance compared with this great dualism.

† The statement in Theophrast. Char. Proem. (worthless as is the authority on which it rests) is probably not far from the truth—πάντων τῶν Ἑλλήνων ὁμοίως παιδευομένων. Cp. Wittmann—Erziehung und Unterricht bei Platon, p. 7.

succeed in mastering the Athenian and Spartan systems of education, we shall be in possession of the main ideas current in the other Hellenic states, although their developement may well have been modified greatly by varying conditions in each individual case.

*The Dorians.* From the numerous and inconsistent legends of the origin of the Dorians, discussed very fully by Ottfried Müller, we can learn but little as to the influences which stamped upon them their well-marked character. It is possible that comparative philology, which has done so much for us already, may yet be able to give us some light on this subject; but at present it can carry us no further than the days when the Italo-Hellenic people were still united.\* We may perhaps conjecture that a life in the rough mountainous country of Northern

---

\* The picture of their common civilisation has been graphically sketched by Mommsen (i. 19–31); the materials for adding a few more details are given by Fick—"Vergleichendes Wörterbuch" (2nd edition), pp. 421–504. I intentionally pass over the difficult question whether the Keltic tribes remained united with the Italians up to and after their separation from the Hellenes. But cp. Peile's "Etymology," 24–27; and Schleicher in Rhein. Mus. for 1859.

Hellas, exposed to the constant assaults of the barbarians who were ever pressing southwards, was the main cause of their distinctive character. Dr. Donaldson, following Kenrick, finds a trace of their earliest home in Greece in the very name *Dorian* (Δωριεῖς, 'Highlanders,' from δα and ὄρος); and the more probable explanation of the name sanctioned by Prof. G. Curtius (vielleicht bedeutete auch Δωρί-ς eigentlich Holzland, Waldland, so dass die Δωριεῖς unsern "Holsaten" entsprächen) points in the same direction. Dr. E. Curtius says, I think with justice, that "in the full and broad sounds of their dialect we seem to recognise the chest strengthened by mountain air and mountain life." But our knowledge of their history before the dawn of trustworthy tradition is too slight to enable us to determine whether it was only external conditions which moulded their national life, or whether there were not far earlier race distinctions which contributed largely to fashion it. It is certain that wherever we come upon them in historic times we find the same characteristic tendencies, obscured, it may be, in wealthy mercantile cities like Corinth (itself, however, to a large extent Achaean), and appearing in their unmixed clearness only in isolated states like Crete, yet nowhere wholly wanting. We have on one side a freshness and simplicity of life, a manly energy, a bright and joyous but self-restrained and calm religion—points on which Müller delights to dwell; but on the other hand, a want of the free play of individual activity, the quick intellectual subtlety, the restless, inquisitive temper of the Ionian mind. Above all we have the great idea of the state dominating every member, and owning their absolute and unqualified obedience. In the vigorous and suggestive passage in which Mommsen compares the Italian and Hellenic characters, he appears to have had in view throughout Athens as the type and crown of Hellas, we cannot say wrongly; but in many points the Dorians approach more nearly to the Italian than to the Athenian character; and their conception of the claims of the state seems to have been one of these. It cannot be said of Dorians that "they sacrificed the whole to its individual elements, the nation to the single state, and the single state to the citizen;" it is rather true that they "surrendered their personal will for the sake of freedom, and learnt to obey their fathers, that they might know how to obey the State," although, "in such subjection as this, individual developement might be arrested, and the germs of the fairest promise in man might be arrested in the bud." It is very noteworthy from this point of view, that the centralising influence of Delphi, if not originating in Dorian ideas, was at least extended by Dorian energy. Prof. Curtius holds that the Dorian idea of a state was formed by the action of the Delphic priesthood. Whether this was the case, or whether it was external pressure that welded the Dorians into greater unity than was ever attained by the looser Ionian city-federations, may be left uncertain. It is clear that throughout the period of the prime of Hellas, there was a very close connection and sympathy between the Del-

<sub>Mommsen, i. 24.</sub>

<sub>Ibid., i. 31.</sub>

phic authorities and the leading Dorian states. And, in spite of the Spartan xenelasy, it is probable that the link of union lay in common Panhellenic tendencies. At any rate we find the great Olympian, Pythian, Nemean, and Isthmian games all celebrated in Dorian territory, and in honour of deities distinctively or especially Dorian.

The key to the right understanding of the Spartan institutions lies in regarding them as the old Dorian laws and customs modified under the pressure of exceptional conditions. The current traditions represented the conquest of Laconia as rapid and complete. But this is sufficiently disproved, not only by isolated fragments of information which are wholly inconsistent with any such view, but also by considering the nature of the case. The Spartans to the end of their history were confessedly very unskilful in the attack of fortified places; and, indeed, how was it possible that their phalanx of spearmen, irresistible in the open field, should be equally adapted to scale the Acro-Corinthus or the Argive

*[margin notes:]*
Cp. Müller's Dorians, ii. 241.

Curtius, ii. 27–29.

*The Spartan institutions.*

See K. F. Hermann's arguments quoted by Grote, Plato, iii. 309.

Müller, book i. cc. 4, 5.

Larisa? It cannot be doubted that the Dorians of Sparta carried on for years, and it may be for generations, a kind of ἐπιτειχισμὸς against the surrounding Achaean towns. Hence their distinguishing belief in the absolute right of the state to the unconditional obedience of its citizens, must have been intensified by the knowledge that this unhesitating devotion was simply needful for self-preservation. Sparta was a garrison planted in the midst of enemies, and its laws and habits were those of a garrison. That every citizen should be trained to the highest perfection of physical condition and discipline was an essential requisite of their position. And when the supremacy of Sparta over Amyclae, Aegys, Pharis, and Helos had once been established, not less vigilance and energy were needed to retain it. The Achaean population was crushed, but not exterminated. *Mutatis mutandis*, the position of the Spartans was not unlike that which the English have for a century held in India. In our own case the maintenance of empire is aided by a more advanced

Cp. Ar. Pol. ii. 9, 2. οἱ Εἵλωτες . . ὥσπερ ἐφεδρεύοντες τοῖς ἀτυχήμασι διατελοῦσιν.

material civilisation, and by a still more marked superiority of national character. But the Dorian invaders were probably decidedly inferior to the Achaeans in the arts of peace, and distinctions of race, though of course existing, were of much less importance than is the case as between the Englishman and the Bengali. But the needful conditions for the rule of a nation by a small body of foreigners are a proud consciousness on the part of the rulers that, man for man, they are immeasurably superior to the subject race, and an unhesitating daring, ready in times of trial to fling itself upon unnumbered enemies μὴ φρονήματι μόνον ἀλλὰ καὶ καταφρονήματι. Like the slave-priest of Aricia, Sparta held her national life only so long as she proved herself stronger in battle than all who might come against her. And as the chance of a struggle was always imminent, every one of her citizens was kept in perfect training for it.

That Lycurgus had a real historical existence hardly admits of doubt. But it is difficult to determine what amount of

---

Compare the words of Brasidas: Thuc. iv. 126; Ar. Pol. ii. 9, 3.

Lycurgus.

Thirlwall, i. 338; Curtius, i. 191.

originality may be ascribed to his legislation. On the whole it seems most probable that he did little more than revive and place under a strong religious sanction the ancient laws and institutions of the Dorians, adapting them in a few particulars to the peculiar position of the Spartans. This is the view of Bishop Thirlwall, accepted on the whole by Curtius.* The basis of all his reforms, as Plutarch tells us, was his system of national education. But here we must digress for a moment to limit the application of the term. In Sparta as in Athens, and indeed throughout Hellas, the phrase bore a very different meaning from that which is happily attached to it in modern times. In Sparta there were at most nine thousand families of citizens,

<small>Plut. Lyc. 14.</small>

---

* I am speaking of course with reference mainly to the social institutions of Lycurgus. There is force in the arguments by which Curtius endeavours to show that part of the political constitution was distinctly Achaean. But it is surprising to find him ignoring the irrefragable evidence by which Grote has disproved the tradition of an equal division of land. To the whole system of Sparta Grote is disposed to attribute more originality and a more exceptional position than most other authorities will allow. Compare his History, and especially his " Plato," vol. iii. 309, note $x$.

surrounded by more than three times as many Perioeci, and a Helot population, amounting on the whole at least to two hundred and fifty thousand. In Attica, with its population of half a million, at least four-fifths of the whole were slaves. But of anything like a public education of slaves, or even of Perioeci, there could never have been a question in Hellas. The "nation" then, in the eyes of a Greek, would only consist of the free population, possessing the full civic rights—Aristotle even excludes the "base mechanicals" (βάναυσοι) from his ideal state—and therefore the term "national education" must be taken in the limited sense of the education of that small minority of the whole community which was recognised as forming the nation. But to resume: the aim of Lycurgus was to train the citizens of Sparta to the greatest possible efficiency in war. To this every other object was unsparingly sacrificed. Plato says in his Laws (I. 630 D) πάντα τά τ' ἐν Λακεδαίμονι καὶ τὰ τῇδε πρὸς τὸν πόλεμον μάλιστα βλέποντας Λυκοῦργόν τε καὶ Μίνω τίθεσθαι τὰ νόμιμα. On the means which he

*Müller, ii. 45.*

*Böckh, Publ. Econ. book i. c. 7.*

employed to obtain this result we have, fortunately, ample and trustworthy information. It is true that the writings of Plutarch require to be used with caution. Living, as he did, long after the time when Sparta had ceased to have any independent national life, his facts are of course given us only on second-hand authority. And Mr. Grote has pointed out another less patent source of possible error. The abortive attempts at reform made by Agis and Cleomenes not only had failed to restore the primitive Spartan constitution, but also had caused the new ideas which their enthusiasm or their policy had announced as constituent parts of the Lycurgan institutions to be accepted by later historians as really such. Plutarch has undoubtedly misled us on the question of the equal distribution of the land; and it would be rash to use without suspicion any assertion of his that is unsupported by better authorities. Isocrates, though a contemporary authority for the period which we have especially to consider, is of little value, because of

*Our authorities.*

the strong hostility to the Lacedaemonians which appears in his writings. But Xenophon and Aristotle can be trusted with less reserve. The Λακεδαιμονίων Πολιτεία of the former has been suspected both in ancient and in modern times, but the arguments against it do not appear to be strong; and the tone of the treatise is just what would be expected from the friend of Agesilaus and the exile of Scillus. There is an evident tendency to apologise for Spartan customs and to prefer them to those of Athens; and though this of itself would not be sufficient to prove the authorship, for it became the fashion to write in this style in the Attic schools of philosophy, yet it tends to confirm the opinion which we should form from external evidence. In the case of Aristotle, we have unfortunately lost his Πολιτεῖαι, in which he gathered the material which was employed in his extant treatise τὰ Πολιτικά; but in the latter work we have not only most instructive criticisms, but also, incidentally, very valuable information on the Spartan laws and customs.

*Marginalia:*
Cp. Paneg. §§ 110–132.

Cp. Weiske's dissertation prefixed to Schneider's edition.

Cp. Zeller, ii. 2, 75, 3.

The authority of both Xenophon and Aristotle has been impugned by Manso, on the ground that neither was himself a Spartan; but the former can have been little less familiar with Spartan institutions than a native citizen, while the careful accuracy of Aristotle is surely beyond the possibility of censure. It is to these two writers, therefore, supplemented by the somewhat numerous allusions in the Laws of Plato, that we shall have mainly to look for guidance.

*Sparta I. ii. 69.*

The absolute right of the State to dispose of its members as seemed to it best was not allowed to remain a theory at Sparta. From their birth through all the successive stages of infancy, childhood, youth, and manhood, its authority never ceased to be seen and felt. In fact it may be said to have commenced even before their appearance in the world; for it was the state which determined what marriages should be sanctioned or forbidden. The numerous regulations as to the time, the manner, and the place of marriage, ascribed by Xenophon to Lycurgus, all had for their

*Authority of the State.*

*Xen. de Rep. Lac. c. i. Aristotle quite approves of this control. Pol. iv. (vii.) 16.*

object the production of the healthiest and most vigorous offspring; and so far was this desire for εὐγονία carried, that, if our authorities do not mislead us, practices the most revolting, fatal to the nobler aspects of marriage, were deliberately permitted in order to secure it. Müller endeavours to exalt the Dorian idea of marriage by comparing it with the views current in Ionian countries, and he is probably right in his comparative estimate; but he is obliged to confess that at Sparta marriage was considered mainly "as a public institution, in order to rear up a strong and healthy progeny to the nation." Plutarch tells us that "new-born children were carried at once to certain tryers, who were elders of the tribe to which the child belonged. Their business was to view the infant carefully, and if they found it stout and well-made, they gave order for its rearing, and allotted to it one of the nine thousand shares of land for its maintenance: but if they found it puny and ill-shaped, they ordered it to be taken to what was called the Apothetae, a sort of chasm under

*Müller, ii. 211 and 301·2.*

*Vol. i. 105 (Clough). Exposure of children.*

Taygetus, as thinking it neither for the good of the child itself, nor for the public interest, that it should be brought up if it did not, from the very outset, appear made to be healthy and vigorous." This fact rests, I believe, only on the authority of Plutarch, and some of the details are probably inaccurate. For instance, the allotment of one share of land stands or falls with the theory of an equal distribution of property by Lycurgus, which Mr. Grote has so brilliantly disproved: but the general fact of the destruction of deformed or weakly children may very well be true.* Plato (Rep. vi. 460 B), and Aristotle (Pol. iv. (vii.) 16, 15), both give their sanction to it; and it seems to have been commonly allowed, if not approved, in Hellas.† Some, however, have interpreted the 'putting away' (ἀπόθεσις) to mean

* Thirlwall does not doubt it, i. 372.
† On the question how far the arbitrary exposure of children was generally practised and approved there are some valuable remarks by K. F. Hermann in "Charikles," ii. 5 (2nd edition). It is noteworthy that at Thebes (but apparently there alone) it was expressly forbidden by law, and provision was made by the State for the support of those children whose parents were unable to keep them. Cp. Aelian. Var. Hist. ii. 7, and Ussing, op. cit. p. 23.

simply that such infants were exposed in the villages of the Perioeci, and grew up among them, excluded from the "military brotherhood" of the Spartans. Up to the age of seven years, children were left to the care of their mothers or of nurses; but the rigorous discipline under which they were to spend their lives began at once. Swaddling bands were discarded, and they grew up unfettered in limb; their food was plain, and not too plentiful; and Plutarch adds the hardly credible information that they were "not afraid in the dark, or of being left alone, without any peevishness or ill-humour or crying." We cannot wonder that Spartan nurses, if they really secured this, "were often bought up or hired by people of other countries," as, for instance, by the parents of Alcibiades.* A glimpse at the brighter side of the children's life is given us by the well-known story of Agesilaus riding on a stick to

<small>Curtius, i. 202.</small>

<small>*Training of young children.*</small>

<small>Plut. Lycurg. 16.</small>

<small>κάλαμον περιβεβηκώς. Plut. Ages, 25.</small>

---

* Schömann, Griech. Alterth. i. 265 (note 2), quotes another instance of a Laconian nurse at Athens, in Malicha of Cythera, nurse to the children of Diogiton. Her tomb has been recently discovered in Athens. Cp. Bulletino di corrisp. Archeol. 1841, p. 56.

amuse his little ones; and to a Dorian, if not to a Spartan, the philosopher Archytas, is ascribed the credit of the invention of the rattle (πλαταγή,) "which they give to children, in order that having the use of this they may not break any of the things in the house: for little creatures cannot keep still." At seven years of age boys were taken from their parents, and the regular education (ἀγωγή) by the State commenced. Xenophon contrasts the custom of the other Greeks in this respect with that of the Spartans; for while the former, as soon as the children could understand what was said to them, placed them in charge of a slave called the παιδαγωγός, and sent them off with him to schoolmasters, Lycurgus chose as their master one of the most eminent of the citizens, to whom he assigned the office of παιδονόμος. The boys were divided into bands called ἀγέλαι, or in the Laconian dialect βοῦαι, and over each of these was a βουάγορ, chosen from the youths who were just entering manhood, who acted as the captain of the band. All, rich and poor

*Arist. Pol. v. (viii.) 6, 2.*

*State education.*

alike, were subjected to the same rigid discipline, and did their exercises and took their play together. A specific quantity of food was allotted to each; but this was intentionally barely sufficient for them, in order that they might learn to do with as little as possible.* At the same time they were encouraged to steal whatever they could, as being so best prepared for military service, "for evidently one who is to play the thief, must watch by night and deceive by day, lie in ambush, ay, and supply himself with spies, if he is to get anything." But any one who was detected in stealing was beaten severely for his clumsiness in not learning aptly, as Xenophon says, the lesson which it was intended to teach him. There was a strange practice of διαμαστίγωσις, according to which boys were flogged severely at the altar of Artemis Orthia, and vied with each other in bearing the blows without a murmur, even though they

*marginalia:* Xen. Rep. Lac. c. 2.

*marginalia:* Cp. Gellius, xi. 18, 17.

*marginalia:* *Flogging.*

---

* Athenaeus, an uncritical and somewhat doubtful authority, tells us (xii. 12) that leanness was so much admired at Sparta, that the boys were inspected every ten days, and any one who seemed too fat was whipped.

sometimes died under the suffering. This was probably first adopted as a substitute for human sacrifices;* a view which is supported by the fact that it lasted down to the days of Cicero (Tusc. Disp. ii. 34), Plutarch (Lycurg. p. 108), and even Pausanias (iii. 16, 6, 7). Plutarch, indeed, assures us that he had himself seen several of the youths endure whipping to death. Whatever its origin, it was taken advantage of by the Spartan legislator to strengthen the contempt of pain, which it was one of his principal objects to implant. For the same reason boys till their twelfth year were only allowed to wear a single sleeveless chiton, exchanged as they advanced in years for a plain rough cloak, which served them all the year round. They commonly went barefooted, and often stripped entirely for their games. In all their amusements, as well as their exercises, they were constantly under the eyes of the older men; and we are told that the latter delighted to stir up quarrels

*Dress.*

---

* Cp. Preller, "Griechische Mythologie," i. 240 (2nd edition).

and disputes among them, "to have a good opportunity of finding out their different characters, and of seeing which would be valiant, which a coward, when they should come to more dangerous encounters." From their twelfth year their training increased in severity; and the several stages between this date and that of manhood, which was fixed at thirty years, were marked by different names, corresponding, probably, though we cannot determine the point exactly, to changes in their forms of education.* The little bands (ἴλαι, subdivisions of the βοῦαι mentioned above) slept together on beds of rushes, which they gathered by the banks of the Eurotas; and to train the boys to greater hardihood, no knives were allowed to be used for cutting them. The favourite amusement was hunting, for which the mountain-forests of Laconia gave abundant facilities, and the Spartan hounds were proverbially famous. But the game seems always to have been pursued on foot; for

*Marginal notes: Training of youths. Hunting.*

---

* σιδεῦναι, μελλείρενες, εἰρενες, σφαιρεῖς. Cp. Müller, ii. 315, 316.

## THE CRYPTEIA.

Xenophon, in his enthusiastic treatise called Κυνηγετικός, makes no mention of horses, nor does he speak of their use in hunting in his book περὶ ἱππικῆς. The evidence on which Müller says that "riding was one of the principal occupations of the youths of Sparta," is very slight and untrustworthy, especially in the face of the admitted inferiority of the Lacedaemonian cavalry.* In fact, Müller himself points out elsewhere that a preference for cavalry, according to the principles of antiquity, was a proof of an unstable and effeminate character, exactly the reverse of that exhibited by the heavy-armed soldiery of the Lacedaemonians. On the other hand, I think that we may fairly accept the explanation which he gives of the much-abused κρυπτεία, an institution which, in the way in which Plutarch (Lyc. 28) describes it, is simply incredible. Megillus, the Spartan interlocutor in Plato's Laws, speaks as follows:

*The Crypteia.*

Cp. Grote, ii. 144.

---

\* The expression of Xenophon (Hell. vi. 4, 10) is qualified: τοῖς δὲ Λακεδαιμονίοις κατ' ἐκεῖνον τὸν χρόνον πονηρότατον ἦν τὸ ἱππικόν, and therefore should not have been referred to by Mr. Mason in his careful article on Exercitus (Greek) in Dict. Ant. to prove the point; but the general fact is unquestioned. Cp. Müller, ii. 257.

"There is, too, the so-called Crypteia, or secret service, in which wonderful endurance is shown; those who are employed in this wander over the whole country by day and by night, and even in winter have not any shoes on their feet, and are without beds to lie on, and have no one to attend them" (p. 633 B). We may fairly view this in the light of another passage where the philosopher, speaking in the character of the Athenian, describes the services which he will require of the "wardens of the country" (ἀγρονόμοι): "Further at all seasons of the year, summer and winter alike, let them survey minutely the whole country, bearing arms and keeping guard, at the same time acquiring a perfect knowledge of every locality. For there can be no more important kind of information than the exact knowledge of a man's own country; and for this, as well as for more general reasons of pleasure and advantage, hunting with dogs and other kinds of sports should be pursued by the young. The service to whom this is committed may be called the secret police [κρυπτοί], or wardens of the country; the name does not much signify, but every one who has the safety of the State at heart will use his utmost diligence in this service" (p. 763 A.B). Mr. Jowett justly notices Vol. iv. p. 21 that the crypteia, as well as the public education, is borrowed by Plato from Sparta. It is not unfair, then, to suppose that at least the main objects of this "secret service" were those on which Plato lays most stress, that the young Spartans might obtain an intimate knowledge of their own country for military purposes; and that their frames might be hardened by exposure and vigorous exercise. Of course it is easy to believe that if, while ranging through the land, they found any traces of conspiracy, or even disaffection, among the Helots, they might resort to severe and treacherous means of repression; but this is a very different thing from Plutarch's view, which makes it out to have been a legalised system of gratuitous assassination.* So

* Cramer, in his "Geschichte der Erziehung," a book

## 26 EDUCATION IN SPARTA.

*Tusc. ii. 14, 34.*

Cicero writes: "Leges Lycurgi laboribus erudiunt iuventutem venando, currendo, esuriendo, sitiendo, algendo, aestuando." And no more than a constant vigilance need be understood by the words of Thucydides (iv. 80-2) ἀεὶ γὰρ τὰ πολλὰ Λακεδαιμονίοις πρὸς τοὺς Εἵλωτας τῆς φυλακῆς πέρι μάλιστα καθεστήκει.

*Fights.*

The words of Megillus immediately preceding those already quoted—τὸ περὶ τὰς

*Legg. p. 633 B.*

καρτερήσεις τῶν ἀλγεδόνων πολὺ παρ' ἡμῖν γιγνόμενον ἐν ταῖς πρὸς ἀλλήλους ταῖς χερσὶ μάχαις—contain a reference to a custom which is described by Cicero (Tusc. Disp. v. 27, 77) as existing in his own days: "Adolescentium greges Lacedaemone vidimus ipsi incredibili contentione certantis pugnis, calcibus, unguibus, morsu denique, cum exanimarentur prius quam victos se faterentur." Pausanias

*iii. 14, 8; cp. ii. 2. μάχονται δὲ καὶ ἐν χερσὶ καὶ ἐμπηδῶντες λάξ, δάκνουσί τε καὶ τοὺς ὀφθαλμοὺς ἀντορύσσουσι.*

gives a still more highly-coloured description, from which it appears that no act of violence was spared to gain the victory in these ferocious contests,* which were

that requires to be used with much caution, identifies the κρυπτεία with the legalisation of κλοπή, but he is probably only following Müller somewhat carelessly.

* Mr. Jowett's translation of Plato's expression by " certain hand-to-hand fights," if not positively incorrect, is

carried on in an island called Platanistas, devoted to the purpose. It is curious, after reading Pausanias's description of the biting and kicking that were sanctioned, the bleeding faces and the eyes torn from their sockets, to turn to Müller's comment that "every unprejudiced reader" must consider it "proved satisfactorily that the chief object of Spartan discipline was to invigorate the bodies of the youth, without rendering their minds at the same time either brutal or ferocious!" We are much more inclined to say, with Aristotle, that the Spartans were rendered brute-like by their hardships (οἱ Λάκωνες θηριώδεις ἀπεργάζονται τοῖς πόνοις.) Vol. ii. p. 327. Pol. v. (viii.) 4, 1.

But we must pass from the general training and discipline of the Spartan boys to their education, in the narrower sense of the term. In the eyes of every Greek, education had to deal with three main subjects—γράμματα, μουσική and τὰ ἐν παλαίστρᾳ, though often the first and second were grouped together under the common name *Education of the boys.*

likely to mislead a reader. The essential point is that no *weapons* were allowed but fists, nails, and teeth.

*Gymnastics.*

*Cp. Plutarch, i. 116 (Clough).*

of μουσική.* To gymnastic exercises the Spartans were passionately devoted, and regarded them, with war and the chase, as the only occupations fit for a freeman. But here a distinction must be sharply drawn between gymnastic exercises and the elaborate training of gymnasts. The ancients never failed to mark the difference, and the Romans, much as they practised the exercises of the Campus Martius, looked with entire disapproval, mingled with contempt, upon professional athletes.† Gymnasia, such as abounded in the other Hellenic states, were unknown in Sparta, and it was rare indeed to find a Spartan distinguishing himself, except in

---

\* Cp. Xen. de Rep. Lac. c. 2. εὐθὺς δὲ πέμπουσιν εἰς διδασκάλων, μαθησομένους καὶ γράμματα, καὶ μουσικήν καὶ τὰ ἐν παλαίστρᾳ: Plat. Alcib. i. 106 E. ἔμαθες γὰρ γράμματα καὶ κιθαρίζειν καὶ παλαίειν. Theages 122 E. οὐκ ἐδιδάξατό σε ὁ πατὴρ καὶ ἐπαίδευσεν ἅπερ ἐνθάδε οἱ ἄλλοι πεπαίδευνται οἱ τῶν καλῶν κἀγαθῶν πατέρων υἱεῖς, οἷον γράμματά τε καὶ κιθαρίζειν καὶ παλαίειν καὶ τὴν ἄλλην ἀγωνίαν;

† Cp. the passages from Plutarch, Seneca, and Silius quoted by Becker and K. F. Hermann in Charikles, ii. 162-164. The difference between gymnastics and the training of athletes is well brought out by Jacobs in his eloquent lecture (Vermischte Schriften, iii. 2, 18): "Erziehung der Hellenen zur Sittlichkeit." Cp. also Prof. Mayor's notes on Quintilian X.

certain forms of competition, in the great athletic festivals. Plutarch gives a curious reason for the prohibition of some kinds of gymnastic contests at Sparta. "Lycurgus," he tells us, "being asked what sort of martial exercises or combats he approved of," answered, "All sorts, except that in which you stretch out your hands," that is acknowledge yourself defeated; because it was held to be unworthy of a Spartan to ask for quarter, even in a peaceful encounter. But a more probable reason is to be found in the fact that the special excellence required for distinction in any particular kind of gymnastics interfered with that perfect developement of all the physical powers which proved of most service in war. Euripides, though no friend to Spartans or their ways, certainly expresses Spartan views in the curious fragment cited from his Αὐτόλυκος by Athenaeus: (Frag. 284 Dind.)

*Cp. Paley, Euripides, i. p. xx.*

> τίς γὰρ παλαίσας εὖ, τίς ὠκύπους ἀνὴρ
> ἢ δίσκον ἄρας ἢ γνάθον παίσας καλῶς
> πόλει πατρῴᾳ στέφανον ἤρκεσεν λαβών;
> πότερα μαχοῦνται πολεμίοισιν ἐν χεροῖν
> δίσκους ἔχοντες ἢ δίχ' ἀσπίδων ποσὶ
> θείνοντες ἐκβαλοῦσι πολεμίους πάτρας;

*The whole fragment (28 lines) is well worth comparing, from this point of view.*

*Gymnasts.* The fulness of flesh (πολυσαρκία) with which we find gymnasts often taunted, was quite opposed to the spare and slender "good condition" εὐεξιά, which, as we have seen above, was especially aimed at by the Lacedaemonians. The disproportionate strengthening of the legs of runners and the shoulders of boxers which Sokrates blames in Xenophon's Symposium (II. 17), would be equally disapproved by them; and the careful attention to food and drink (though not always according to the rules of modern "training") which was required of athletes, would have run counter to the first principles of Spartan education. Hence, just as we are told of Philopoemen by Plutarch,* that he put a stop, as far as he could, to athletics in Achaea, so the Lacedaemonians refused to sanction any special gymnastic training. "They appointed no masters to instruct their boys in wrestling, that they might contend, not in sleights of art and little tricks, but in

---

\* οὐ μόνον αὐτὸς ἔφυγε τὸ πρᾶγμα καὶ κατεγέλασεν, ἀλλὰ καὶ στρατηγῶν ὕστερον ἀτιμίαις καὶ προπηλακισμοῖς, ὅσον ἦν ἐπ' αὐτῷ, πᾶσαν ἄθλησιν ἐξέβαλεν ὡς τὰ χρησιμώτατα τῶν σωμάτων εἰς τοὺς ἀναγκαίους ἀγῶνας ἄχρηστα ποιοῦσαν.

strength and courage." It is a little perplexing to find, in the face of Plutarch's repeated statements that Lycurgus forbade boxing as an exercise,* that in Plato (Protag. 342 B) the Laconizers in the various Greek towns "get their ears battered in boxing," in imitation of the Spartans, "and bind the cestus round their arms, and are devoted to gymnastics and wear short cloaks, just as though it were by means of these things that the Lacedaemonians were masters of Greece." But, as in other passages where the "Laconomania" is mentioned,† there is no reference to gymnastics, it is possible that Plato had in his eye certain individual Laconizers whose zeal outstripped their knowledge, and who were no more to be taken as fair representatives of Spartan customs, than some Anglomaniac devotees of *le sport* are to be considered as reproducing the field of the Pytchley or the Quorn. The boxing of which Xenophon

<sup>Plutarch, Apophth. Lac. (vol. i. p. 434 Goodwin).</sup>

<sup>Rep. Lac. iv. 6.</sup>

---

\* Plutarch, Lyc. 19. Reg. Apophth. 125. Lac. Apophth. 225 (Müller, ii. 320).

† Cp. Aristoph. Av. 1282 (with Kock's note). Demosth. in Con. 1267. Plut. Phoc. 10.

speaks does not appear to have been an exercise, but an angry fight. Gladiators, too (ὁπλόμαχοι), were forbidden at Sparta,* partly because the legislator does not seem to have wished to encourage their special training, but also, we may well believe, because the use of arms was thought too serious a thing to be allowed for mere amusement. But all gymnastic exercises which had for their object the harmonious developement of all the bodily powers were pursued with eagerness. In wrestling especially they excelled, and Xenophon tells us that they were noted for all forms of it alike, though it is not easy to identify the various descriptions which he mentions. All their exercises were carried on under the eyes, not only of their appointed superintendent, but also of as many of the older citizens as chose to be present, and the emulation thus inspired was regarded as one of the most powerful motives that could be brought

*Wrestling.*

Cp. Rep. Lac. vi. 9, with Schneider's note.

* Plato Laches, 183 B. τοὺς ἐν ὅπλοις μαχομένους ἐγὼ τούτους ὁρῶ τὴν μὲν Λακεδαίμονα ἡγουμένους εἶναι ἄβατον ἱερὸν καὶ οὐδὲ ἄκρῳ ποδὶ ἐπιβαίνοντας, κ.τ.λ.

to bear upon the youthful warrior. By this means also boys, in what might be considered their hours of amusement, were made to feel the continual presence of a restraining power;—for every adult citizen was regarded as possessing a father's full authority over the children of the State, an authority which, in the absence of the usual Pædonomus, he might enforce by blows. And as most of these exercises seem to have been performed by the troops (ἴλαι) together and under a common command, they must have greatly tended to produce the effect at which the Spartan education was always aiming, to lead the individual citizen to feel himself always closely encompassed by a system of rigid rules, and as nothing in himself, except so far as he formed a unit in a perfect whole. Xen. Rep. Lac. vi. 2.

The same sense of "solidarity" must have been powerfully strengthened by the choral dances, which were constantly practised. The broad distinction between the passionate outpourings of the fiery Lesbian school and the grave high choric songs of Alcman and Terpsichorus bears witness Choric dances.

Cp. Curtius, ii. 82.

to a deep distinction between the tribes for whom they wrote. And the contrast is not less great between the iambics and elegiacs of the Ionian bards and the spirit-stirring paeans and hyporchemes that were welcome in Lacedaemon. As "the vital principle of the Lacedaemonian constitution was harmony, a complete unity of interests and feeling among the members of the privileged class, an absorption in fact, to this extent, of the individual in the mass," so the powerful aid given to this by the song and dance of the chorus could not be overlooked. The graceful and ordered motion of the body in the dance was of itself no slight assistance to military training;* but the habit of acting rapidly in numbers in obedience to a leader must have been of still more value. Hence we are prepared to find the origin of the Pyrrhich dance attributed to Sparta; and although other authorities gave different accounts on this point, it is certain that

<small>Mure, iii. 47.</small>

<small>Cp. Plato, Legg. 796 B, and other authorities in Müller, ii. 349.</small>

---

\* Cp. the poet Socrates (apud Athen. xiv. p. 628), supposed by Müller (ii. 342 n.) to be the philosopher.

οἳ δὲ χοροῖς κάλλιστα θεοὺς τιμῶσιν, ἄριστοι ἐν πολέμῳ.

it was nowhere so long\* and ardently practised. Lucian describes a dance of the Spartan ephebi, in which they were ranged in rows one behind another, and danced to the music of the flute, first military and then choral dances, chanting invocations to Aphrodite, or exhortations addressed to each other. In the Gymnopaedia the combination of gymnastic exercises and mimetic dances seems to have reached its fullest developement; and for this time only the customary exclusiveness of Sparta was relaxed, for we hear of great numbers of strangers flocking from all parts to see the festivities. The ὅρμος was a favourite dance, in which youths and girls joined together, linking hand in hand.

Lucian de Salt., 10, 11. Cp. Mure, ii 128.

Xen. Mem. 2, 61, &c.

But the subject of the choral dances naturally leads us to the second great branch of a Spartan education, that which was concerned with the mental and moral training of the children; for the music and song with which the dance was accompanied formed one of the most important

*Music.*

---

\* Athenaeus says that it was danced at Sparta in his own time (circ. A.D. 230).

elements in this. It is not needful for the present purpose that we should plunge into the technical and complicated mysteries of ancient Greek music. It is sufficient for us to note that music was ever regarded among the ancients—and especially among the Greeks—as possessing a very powerful moral influence for good or evil. The music that should be allowed at Sparta was subject to the severest official control: while all the citizens were trained to take their part in the choric songs, the measures to which these should be set were strictly limited to grave and simple strains. The Dorian style was always the favourite one,* though other styles do not appear to have been forbidden. But when a player named Phrynis attempted to perform on a lyre with more than the lawful number of strings, one of the ephors at once de-

---

* As able ἀκόυοντας διατίθεσθαι καθεστηκότως μάλιστα πρὸς ἐτέραν (Ar. Pol. v. 6, 22). " The Dorian mode created a settled and deliberate resolution, exempt alike from the desponding and from the impetuous sentiments. . . . . The marked ethical effects produced by these modes in ancient times are facts perfectly well attested, however difficult they may be to explain on any general theory of music."—Grote, '' History," ii. 190.

stoyed the superfluous chords. A similar story is told of Timotheus, but it rests on very doubtful evidence. Aristotle remarks that the Spartans, "though they do not learn, are yet able to judge correctly, as they assert, what strains are good and what are not good:" οὐ μανθάνοντες ὅμως δύνανται κρίνειν ὀρθῶς, ὥς φασί, τὰ χρηστὰ καὶ τὰ μὴ χρηστὰ τῶν μελῶν (Pol. v. (viii.) 5, 7); but this assertion of their neglect of the study of music must evidently be taken with some limitation: either he is thinking of skill in playing musical instruments, in which case his remark may well be true of the great majority of the citizens; or it may be, as Müller supposes, that in Aristotle's time, "the number of the citizens in Sparta was so greatly diminished, and war occupied so much of the public attention, that the favourable side of Spartan discipline was cast into the shade." But the former supposition is the more probable; for the choric songs of the Spartans would naturally require much less individual skill in playing instruments than the elegies and scolia, which, as we

Cp. Porson in the Museum Criticum, vol. i. p. 506.

Cp. Grote, iii. 73; Dorians, ii. 342.

*Intellectual training.*

shall hereafter see, were common in the Ionian States.*

Whether the Spartan boys received any other mental training than that implied in the study of their choric songs is a point on which our authorities and critics are at variance. Mr. Grote speaks of them as "destitute even of the elements of letters," and bases his opinion mainly upon two passages in the Panathenaicus of Isocrates. In one of these the fact is directly asserted (p. 277): οὗτοι δὲ τοσοῦτον ἀπολελειμμένοι τῆς κοινῆς παιδείας καὶ φιλοσοφίας εἰσὶν ὥστε οὐδὲ γράμματα μανθάνουσιν: in another the belief which Isocrates (rightly or wrongly) held is shown, Mr. Grote thinks, more unmistakeably, because unconsciously, by the words (p. 285): "the most rational Spartans will approve this discourse, if they find any one to read it to them." But surely if Isocrates was capable of a rhetorical exaggeration, which, as Mr. Grote

* Schömann however (Griechische Alterth. I.² 268) holds that they were taught both the lyre and the flute, quoting Chamaeleon (apud Athen. iv. 84, p. 184) as an evidence for the latter at any rate; and rejecting the relevance of the anecdote in Plutarch: Apophth. Lac. 39.

himself allows, deprives his testimony of much of its weight, he was capable also of the rhetorical artifice of dropping a sneer, such as is contained in the second passage, in the hope that it would sting the more for being apparently so unpremeditated. Nor can we suppose that in this "wonderful effusion of senile self-complacency" Isocrates was more careful to observe historic accuracy than in his elaborate Panegyricus, which teems with blunders or exaggerations. Certainly a couple of careless phrases, dropped by a garrulous rhetorician in his ninety-fifth year, ought not to be allowed to outweigh the evidence drawn from the constant references in Herodotus, Thucydides, and Xenophon to written letters and treatises, without the slightest hint that there was any difficulty in reading them, and from the unbroken silence of Plato and Aristotle. Plutarch's evidence that Lycurgus taught the Spartans letters, "in so far as they were required for useful and necessary purposes," may not in itself carry great weight; but the well-established practice of using the scytale

<small>Dr. Thompson, Phaedrus, p. 177.</small>

as a means of communication between the Spartan authorities at home and their generals and ambassadors, cannot be explained away. In short, it appears to me that Colonel Mure (Vol. iii. App. K and N) has gained a victory over Mr. Grote all along the line; and that we are bound to admit at least as much literary culture on the part of the Spartans as is implied in the words of Plutarch.* But this is confessedly very little; and in all but the taste for choric poetry the Spartans must have held as low a position in this respect as was ever occupied by any semi-civilised nation.

*Moral training.*

Their moral training was cared for far more sedulously, and though its range was narrow and defective, within its limits it appears, at all events in the better days of Sparta, to have been crowned with signal success. The virtues which made a man an accomplished warrior and a

* Mr. Grote in his "Plato" somewhat qualifies the assertions made in his History, and asserts only that "the *public training* of youth at Sparta, equal for all the citizens, included nothing of letters and music, which in other cities were considered to be the characteristics of an educated Greek, though probably individual Spartans, more or fewer, acquired these accomplishments for themselves," vol. iii. 307; cp. vol. iii. p. 174.

devoted citizen were impressed upon the Spartan boys by all the resources of an elaborate system of national education; habits formed from his earliest years, the keenest emulation, the most consistent and ever-present public opinion, the entire exclusion of any disturbing element, were all brought to bear upon the future citizen to make him obedient, frugal, brave, and self-denying. And the success of this educational policy, so long as the system of Lycurgus was preserved in secure isolation, was complete. All the qualities requisite to gain dominion were attained as they never have been since. But of the qualities that are needed to make it a blessing instead of a curse to the subjects, of an enlightened and far-seeing liberality, an even-handed justice, a wise and kindly tolerance, we nowhere find the existence, or the desire for their existence. The admirers of Sparta found abundant material for their panegyrics. Xenophon delights to describe the Spartan youths as "walking along the streets with their hands folded in their cloaks, proceeding in silence,

*Its defects.*

De Rep. Lac. c. iii.

looking neither to the right hand nor to the left, but with their eyes modestly fixed upon the ground. There the male sex showed their inherent superiority to the female sex, even in modesty. They were as silent as statues; their eyes as immovable as bronzes, their looks more shamefast than a maiden in the bridal chamber." Plutarch contrasts their brief sententiousness and reverence for their elders with the loquacity and petulance of the Athenian striplings. But we can never forget that when the time of trial came, and Sparta had wrested the reins of empire from Athens, her failure to hold them and to guide them wisely was far more speedy and ignominious than that of her rival. The obedience to law which had been inculcated in the vale of the Eurotas, was forgotten as soon as the Spartan generals passed into a wider field: the simplicity and scorn of luxury, which the whole of their training had been intended to produce, was changed into a venality and greed for gold almost unparalleled. Brasidas was cut off too soon to show what he might have become, but even his brilliant career was tainted with scandalous duplicity; of Agesilaus we know but little, except from absurdly inflated panegyrics; but Pausanias, Gylippus, Lysander, and many others show the same fatal weakness in the presence of temptation. Rarely has a more magnificent opportunity been offered to any state than that which was given to Sparta after the battle of Aegospotami and the submission of Athens; and rarely has such an opportunity been more brutally and wantonly abused. And the secret of it lay in this: that the Spartan national education trained citizens for Sparta and not for Hellas. The duties of a man to his State were diligently taught; the duties of man to man were passed over in silence. How clearly the great philosophical critics of Athens perceived these faults we shall see hereafter. We must now turn our attention to two *subsidia* of the Spartan system of education, which contributed powerfully to mould it. The legislator fully recognised and attempted to regulate

Thuc. iv. 122, 6.

Cp. Cramer, Geschichte der Erziehung, i. 171, note.

# 44 EDUCATION IN SPARTA.

*Influence of lovers.*

the influence exerted on the character of the young by strong personal attachments, and by the power of woman. The relations which commonly existed in Greece between a full-grown man and some favourite boy present us with a curious and often perplexing subject of inquiry. The question is one which must be looked at wholly from a Hellenic stand-point. For the union of Mediaeval Catholicism with the old Teutonic reverence for woman gave birth to a spirit of chivalry, which has, happily, never died out of the world in later days. But the influence of this makes it far more difficult for us to throw ourselves back in thought into the times when it was not yet born. Yet it is certain that to a Greek ardent feelings of devoted attachment to beauty of form and soul were more readily excited by a boy than by a woman.

Cp. the passages quoted by Hermann, Privatalt. p. 232, 2.

Marriage was regarded as a civic duty: and the wife as the mother of legitimate children: the connection with a Hetaera was mainly a matter of sensual pleasure: but it was the passion for a beautiful boy that was looked upon as the source of the noblest inspiration, and as the keenest spur to glorious deeds. The Phaedrus and the Symposium of Plato become intelligible to us only as we read them in the light of this Hellenic sentiment; and the accounts which we have of the relation of Socrates to youths like Alcibiades show us how pure and elevating the attachment might be. It is needless to touch upon the foul and degrading vices which often attended it: it is important for our present purpose only to notice that it was neither originally nor invariably evil. And so far as we can determine from our authorities, the custom, as it was observed in Sparta, was wholly free from the corruptions which sometimes accompanied it in Athens, and which made it in Rome the source of the most shameless abominations. The elder Spartan citizens were encouraged to link themselves by the closest ties of affection to particular boys or youths; it was regarded as disgraceful if a boy found no one to take him under his special protection; and it was a reproach to a man if he neglected this portion of his civic duties. But the

*Cp. Grote's Plato, ii. 206 sqq. The whole subject is discussed with exhaustive fulness by Becker, Charikles, ii. 199–231, and by Jacobs, Vermischte Schriften, iii.*

*Cp. Cic. apud Serv. ad Verg. Aen. x. 325.*

names that were given to the lover and the loved one bear sufficient witness to the lofty conception of their mutual relation. The former was called εἰσπνήλας, he whose task it was to breathe into the soul of his chosen one the spirit of valour and virtue: the latter was the ἀΐτας or hearer, who had to listen to the words of counsel and encouragement. If a man had entered into such a connection, he became responsible to the State for the conduct of his *protégé*, and we are told by Plutarch that a lover was fined by a magistrate, because the lad whom he loved cried out in a cowardly fashion while he was fighting. But to allow any sensual taint to enter into this attachment was considered as extremely disgraceful; and we are assured by several respectable authorities, that no jealousy was felt if one man had several favourites, or one boy many lovers. We have no right then to regard this feature of the Spartan system as anything but the legal recognition of what was an inspiring aid to the attainment of the standard of virtue aimed at.

*Marginalia:* Lycurg. c. 18. / Xen. Rep. Lac. 2, 13. Cp. Charikles, ii. 221–223; Schömann, Gr. Alterth. i. 270; Cic. Rep. iv. 4.

The same remark is probably true of the relation of the sexes as established by Lycurgus. The main object of the training to which he subjected girls as well as boys—an object which is stated frequently by Xenophon and Plutarch with a directness little suited to modern feelings—was that they might produce vigorous offspring. To this end he established a discipline for girls, of which we have but fragmentary notices, but which seems to have differed but little from that prescribed for boys. There was, probably, the same division into bands and troops, the same constant supervision by a magistrate of high rank, the same simple fare and scanty dress, the same rigid training in gymnastics, dancing, and singing. But what excited most astonishment on the part of the Ionian Greeks, accustomed as they were to the seclusion of women in the inner chambers, and to the long and graceful Ionian χιτών, was the free mixture of youths and girls in the amusements of the games, and the exposure of the latter, which was not only

*Influence of women.*

sanctioned but encouraged. Plutarch speaks as if the girls exercised entirely naked, but they seem from other authorities to have worn a σχιστός χιτών, reaching to the knee, and open on either side. In any case, the object of the lawgiver was to train his citizens to such healthy freedom of intercourse with the other sex that prurient thoughts might be excluded by the absence of any attractive attempts at concealment; and that youths and maidens might mix together in pure simplicity. The experiment was hazardous, but the unanimous voice of all our authorities bears witness to its success in this instance. The tone of morality at Sparta would bear comparison with that of any other city of Hellas: we find no reference to a class of prostitutes: adultery was all but unknown, and jealousy extremely rare. Love-matches were common, and we have several instances of the most devoted conjugal affection. It is true that Aristotle gives a picture far from attractive of the luxury, pride, and wealth of the Spartan women of his own

*[margin notes: Charikles, ii. 173–175. Cp. Müller's Denkm. ii. 118. Cp. Schömann, II.² 271. Grote, ii. 151; Müller, ii. 303–305; Pol. ii. 6, 5.]*

time; but we cannot but believe that the philosopher is generalising hastily from a few notorious instances; and, in one point of his criticism, his censures of the cowardice which he thinks they showed during the invasion of Laconia by Epaminondas, he is clearly unfair to them. On the whole, it appears that the splendid vigour and beauty, which was universally ascribed to the Spartan women,* was not purchased at the cost of maidenly purity and decorum. But the interest in manly accomplishments which their whole training gave to them, must have added great weight to their influence with the youths; and the hope of distinguishing himself under their eyes in gymnastic contests, must have been one of the most powerful incentives to a youthful Spartan. It was the crowning point of the Lacedaemonian training that, at solemn feasts, the maidens stood around, "now and then making by jests a befitting reflection upon those who had misbehaved themselves in the wars, and again sing-

<small>Plutarch (i. 101, Clough) is indignant at the misrepresentations of Aristotle.</small>

---

* To this we have frequent reference in the Lysistrata.

ing encomiums upon those who had done any gallant action; and by these means inspiring the younger sort with an emulation of their glory. Those who were thus commended went away proud, elated, and gratified with their honour among the maidens; and those who were rallied were as sensibly touched with it as if they had been formally reprimanded; and so much the more, because the kings and the elders, as well as the rest of the city, saw and heard all that passed."

<small>Plutarch, i. 102 (Clough).</small>

<small>Athenian opinions of this system.</small> Such is a general sketch of the theory and practice of national education at Sparta. Its errors and defects have been occasionally noted in passing; but these brief notices may now be supplemented by a somewhat more complete consideration of the question, What was the judgment of contemporaneous Hellas on the system?

<small>Cp. Mem. iii. 5, 15, 12, 5. But this strong Spartan tone disappears in his latest work, De Vect. Athen. Cp. Grote's Plato, iii. 601.</small> Some there were, like Xenophon, who viewed it with an unmodified admiration. Nowhere in his treatise do we find a trace of criticism. He strikes the keynote in the first few lines: "Lycurgus, who gave them the laws whereby they

grew to prosperity, I greatly admire, and hold to have been extremely wise" (εἰς τὰ ἔσχατα μάλα σοφὸν ἡγοῦμαι), and from this he never deviates. Nor does he ever give a hint that the success of this belauded legislation had been less than might have been expected; for the chapter "de depravata Lycurgi disciplina" bears the plainest marks of spuriousness. But the ordinary judgment was not so favourable. ✓ The way in which the Spartan system was looked upon by a cultivated Athenian may be gathered from the magnificent speech of Pericles, in Thucydides (II. 35-47). Whether the words employed are those of the orator or those of the historian matters but little for our present purpose. Thucydides is at least as good an authority as Pericles for the general tone of feeling at Athens. We find in the Funeral Speech, throughout the earlier chapters, an under-current of allusion to Spartan practices, with which the Athenian customs are contrasted. The original and autochthonous nature of the Athenian constitution, the absence of any disabili-

<sub>Cp. Thuc. i. 22, 1.</sub>

ties arising from birth or fortune, the spirit of liberty which regulated every act of public or private life, the ready toleration of varying habits and pursuits, the freedom from sour and censorious looks, the willing obedience from a sense of honour to the national code, written or understood, all are points in which Athens is praised, and Sparta implicitly disparaged. The orator dwells on their full enjoyment of the festivities, which the Dorians ridiculed, and of the luxuries of every clime, attracted to their capital by its splendour and its fortunate position. Strangers are gladly welcomed, and alien acts unknown. Their fondness for art is free from extravagance, their love of letters does not disable them for war or business. Above all, they do not, as their rivals do, set out in pursuit of manly prowess by a long and toilsome process of training; yet, though living at their ease, they are as ready to meet dangers as any one, happily combining chivalrous daring with a careful calculation of the expedient course. And thus a double advantage is gained; they do not suffer from the dread of impending dangers, nor do they yield in courage to the slaves of a life-long drill. Whatever the pedant might say, the practical statesman had little doubt that the boasted system of Lycurgus sacrificed the noblest parts of the nature of man to secure in lower regions a superiority that was at best but doubtful. Though here the orator does less than justice to Lacedaemon. Whether the cost was not too great at which her pre-eminence in arms was purchased, is another question; but it cannot be doubted that it was recognised and admitted as a rule in Greece; and few were ashamed to confess themselves inferior in military skill and discipline to the consummate craftsmen and professors of military science (ἄκροι τεχνῖται καὶ σοφισταὶ τῶν πολεμικῶν). Cp. Grote, ii. 214, 215.

Plato seems to have been strongly attracted by the ordinances of Lycurgus. They furnished him a concrete instance on which to base his ideal structure. At Sparta that absolute supremacy of the State in every detail of the life of the *Plato's admiration.*

citizen, which he laid down as his fundamental postulate, was actually carried into effect. As Mr. Grote says, to an objector who had asked him how he could possibly expect that individuals would submit to such an unlimited interference as that which he enjoined in his Republic, he would have replied: "Look at Sparta. You see there interference as constant and rigorous as that which I propose, endured by the citizens, not only without resistance, but with a tenacity and long continuance such as is not found among other communities with more lax regulations. The habits and sentiments of the Spartan citizen are fashioned to these institutions. Far from being anxious to shake them off, he accounts them a necessity as well as an honour." But though he had much sympathy with the Spartan institutions, and based his own schemes, as stated in the Republic and the Laws, more upon them than upon any other existing system, still he was not wholly blind to its defects.* His criti-

Plato, iii. 210.

* Mr. Jowett defines the Republic as "the Spartan con-

cisms are to be found mainly in the first *Plato's criticisms.* book of the Laws, where the Athenian examines the constitutions of Crete and P. 633. Sparta. The principal points of his censure are the preference of war to peace, and the direction thus given to the whole course of education, the neglect of music in favour of gymnastic exercises, the license which existed among the Spartan women, and the yet greater P. 637 B. evils which arose from the close intimacy of the gymnasia and the common feasts. He pronounces that Lacedaemon P. 636. had no institutions to strengthen her citizens against the temptations of pleasure, and that the value of festive intercourse, as a revealer of the character of men, was wholly lost sight of. In the second book he finds fault with the exclusive attention paid to choral music: "Your young men," he says to Megillus, the Spartan, "are like wild colts, feeding in a herd together; no one takes the individual colt and rubs him down, and

stitution appended to a government of philosophers" (Plato, iv. 20), and there is as much truth in this as there usually is in an epigram.

tries to give him the qualities which would make him a statesman as well as a soldier." They ought to have been taught that courage was not the first of the virtues, as Tyrtaeus had ranked it, but only the fourth, and lowest among the cardinal virtues. On the other hand, Plato heartily commends in the Spartan system of national education the importance attached to obedience, and the slight regard for wealth, the care taken of marriages, and the reverence paid to elders.

What his own views were on the training of the youth of a nation, we shall have to consider more fully hereafter.

*Aristotle's criticisms.*

Aristotle in his criticism of the Spartan constitution (Polit. II. 9) touches but slightly on the method of education; but he fully accepts the judgment of Plato, as expressed in his Laws, that fault may be justly found with the fundamental principle (ὑπόθεσις) of the legislator, inasmuch as the whole system of his laws is directed towards the cultivation of a part only of virtue, that which secures supremacy in war. Hence, as he says, "they

Pol. ii. 9, 34.

were preserved in a healthy condition while they were at war, but they fell into ruin when they had won the supremacy (ἐσώζοντο μὲν πολεμοῦντες, ἀπώλλυντο δὲ ἄρξαντες). In another passage he censures their extreme devotion to gymnastics, which left their children untaught in all the points essential to man, the most necessary rudiments of intellectual training; thus, λίαν εἰς ταῦτα ἀνέντες τοὺς παῖδας, καὶ τῶν ἀναγκαίων ἀπαιδαγωγήτους ποιήσαντες βαναύσους κατεργάζονται κατά γε τὸ ἀληθές. But it is noteworthy that the other main point in which the Spartan national education seems so defective to the judgment of modern Christian Europe, namely, that so large a portion of the nation was excluded from its benefits, is specially chosen out by Aristotle for approval. For, he says, freedom from the necessity of attention to the first requisites of life on the part of the citizens, is one of the most important notes of a well-organized community. A subject population, living in ignorant slavery or serfage, is regarded by him with a complacency which is strangely foreign to our own ideas of justice.

Pol. v. (viii.) 4, 5.

Pol. ii. 9, 2.

Only, he adds, it is difficult to know how to deal with such; for if you treat them kindly they wax wanton, but if they are treated with severity you must always be on your guard against conspiracy and revolt. The account which Aristotle gives us of the cowardly, domineering, and avaricious spirit engendered in the Spartan women, by what he considers their lax and disorderly training, has been already touched upon.

On the general question of Spartan education there is little to be added from our modern stand-point to the criticisms of the philosophers of Athens. The evils arising from a discipline so narrow in its aims and so unnatural in its processes, cannot be felt or described more forcibly than was the case with Plato and Aristotle. But we may be permitted to notice one point on which they do not dwell. It was death to a Spartan to leave his country without permission; and this is a significant fact. The Spartan discipline was possible only so long as all the citizens subjected to it were kept

*Further defects.*

## ITS DEFECTS.

in narrow isolation from the rest of Hellas. The ξενηλασία of Lacedaemon, which seemed so repulsive to the rest of the Greeks, was simply a needful measure of self-preservation. In the presence of those who lived by other and laxer rules, a Spartan felt bewildered; the only law he knew was the law of his country, and if strangers had been permitted to settle in Laconia the same result must have followed there which we find in almost every case in which a Spartan was absent for any long time from his fatherland. The ties of the law in which he had been educated were broken, and no others were found to take their place; so that he fell into a lawlessness which was rarely if ever rivalled by the citizens of less rigidly organized communities. Not only were the aims of the Spartan education low and unworthy, but also they required for their attainment external conditions which were wholly inconsistent with the free and full developement of the life of the nation and of the individual citizens.

Cp. Curtius, i. 204, and again i. 211.

## CHAPTER II.

### NATIONAL EDUCATION AT ATHENS.

*Athens compared with Sparta.*

E pass into a wholly different air when we turn from the banks of the Eurotas to the slopes of Hymettus. The sun is as bright and the breeze as healthy; but there is a dainty clearness in the sky\* that was wanting in the shadow of Taygetus, and the many-dimpling sparkle of the ocean seems to lend a brightness to the heaven under which it is smiling. As the lofty mountain-wall which hems in Laconia on every side but that which is guarded by a cliff-bound coast seemed destined to preserve the Spartans in a

---

\* The infinite charm of the Athenian air has been nowhere more gracefully set forth than by Dr. Newman, "Historical Sketches," pp. 20–22.

rigid isolation, so the "highway of the nations," to which the peninsular form and excellent harbours of Attica gave such easy access, appeared to attract its autochthonous people to a richly-cultured and manifold life. As in the garrison-city of Sparta the State held absolute lordship over every citizen, from the cradle to the grave, so—

*Cp. Pictet, Les Aryas Primitifs, i. 115, and G. Curtius, Grundzüge, 354.*

> Where on the Ægean shore the city stood,
> Built nobly,

the true Hellenic principle of the fullest and freest developement of the individual, ruled every civic ordinance. It is evident that a national system of education, in the strictest sense of the term, would have been wholly foreign to the genius of the State. To force every citizen from childhood into the same rigid mould, to crush the play of the natural emotions and impulses, and to sacrifice the beauty and joy of the life of the agora, or the country home, to the claims of military drill, were aims which were happily rendered needless by the position of Attica, as well as distasteful to the Athenian temperament.

*No State education at Athens.*

And yet, on the other hand, we are not to suppose that — at least in the better days of the State — the liberty which was readily conceded was allowed to pass into unrestricted license. If the methods by which a father should train his children were not rigidly prescribed by the State, at least the object to be attained was set before him, and not only the force of public opinion, but also the positive control of law and judicial authority, was brought to bear on him to secure its accomplishment. If there was no common discipline, at least there were definite laws requiring that every child should be trained in the two great branches of Greek education, μουσική and γυμναστική. And so long as it retained its original powers, the court of Areopagus was charged with the enforcement of the laws in this respect. Quintilian (v. 9, 13) tells us that they even condemned to death a boy who had torn out the eyes of his quails; and according to Athenaeus (iv. 6) two youths were brought up before them, charged with attending the lectures of philosophers

*(margin: Plato, Crito, 50 E.)*

*(margin: Isocrates complains bitterly of the disuse of this supervision on the part of the Areopagus.)*

without having any visible livelihood. Instances like this, which might be multiplied, show that the supervision exercised was not merely nominal.

At first children were left wholly to the care of their mothers and nurses, and the diligence of scholars like Becker and Hermann has gathered many interesting particulars of their modes of training. Toys of many kinds are mentioned—rattles (see p. 18), toy carts,* and beds, dolls of wax and clay, hoops, and tops; several games are noticed, such as flying cockchafers and blind-man's buff; † and stories of various kinds, terrific or amusing, were employed to frighten the children out of mischief,‡ or to keep them in good humour. As soon as the children grew too old to

*Amusements of children.*

Cp. Hermann, Privatalterth. pp. 261–268.

Cp. Ar. Nub. 763 (Kock), and Schol. on Vesp. 1341.

---

\* Ar. Nub. 863; cp. 877–881.

† Cp. Pollux, ix. 122. ἡ δὲ χαλκῆ μυῖα, ταινίᾳ τὼ ὀφθαλμὼ περισφίγξαντες ἑνὸς παιδός, ὁ μὲν περιστρέφεται κηρύττων· χαλκῆν μυῖαν θηράσω· οἱ δὲ ἀποκρινάμενοι, θηράσεις ἀλλ' οὐ λήψει, σκύτεσι βυβλίνοις παίουσιν αὐτόν, ἕως τινὸς αὐτῶν λήψεται. (For ὀστρακίνδα cp. Phaedr. 241 B with Dr. Thompson's note).

‡ Chrysippus blames those who would deter men from sin by the fear of punishment from the gods—ὡς οὐδὲν διαφέροντας τῆς 'Ακκοῦς καὶ τῆς 'Αλφιτοῦς, δι' ὧν τὰ παιδάρια τοῦ κακοσχολεῖν αἱ γυναῖκες ἀπείργουσιν.

*The slave-attendants.*

be managed any longer by their mothers and nurses, they were placed under the care of παιδαγωγοί.* The primary duty of these slave-attendants was to conduct the children to the public schools, but they had also entrusted to them a general supervision of their conduct, and especially of their manners and deportment (εὐκοσμία); and they appear even to have inflicted personal chastisement.† They would be naturally chosen from the most honest and trusted members of the household, but as a rule they possessed little or no literary accomplishments themselves. Plutarch is very indignant at the careless-

---

* Cp. an amusing passage in Lucian Hermotim. 82 : ἐπεὶ καὶ αἱ τίτθαι τοιάδε λέγουσι περὶ τῶν παιδίων, ὡς ἀπιτέον αὐτοῖς ἐς διδασκάλου· καὶ γὰρ ἂν μηδέπω μαθεῖν ἀγαθόν τι δύνωνται, ἀλλ' οὖν φαῦλον οὐδὲν ποιήσουσιν ἐκεῖ μένοντες. Cp. Ussing, Darstellung, &c. pp. 68–73, and Lightfoot on Gal. iii. 24.

† The παιδαγωγεῖον mentioned by Demosthenes (de Cor. p. 313) was probably a waiting-room, devoted to the use of the slave-attendants [so Hermann in Charikles, ii. p. 21 and Simcox, *ad loc.*]; Mr. Holmes (with Pollux, iv. 19) takes it to mean simply the schoolroom, but this meaning weakens the force of the passage ; and is there any authority for his assertion that παιδαγωγὸς sometimes is used in the wider sense of "tutor?" All the instances of this usage that I have been able to discover, belong to a later time than that of Demosthenes. (Cp. Hermann, Privatalterth. p. 276, 19).

ness which some parents in his day showed in the choice of their "pedagogues," entrusting the care of their children only to such slaves as were unfit for any other occupation.* The age at which the children were committed to the pedagogues cannot have been fixed very rigidly; much would depend upon their own character and development, and much upon the position of their parents; for, as Plato says (Protagor. p. 326), the sons of rich men would go to school earlier than those of others, and remain there longer. But from several passages of Plato and Aristotle it seems probable that the usual age for commencing to attend school was about seven years, and that for two or three years after that the children learnt little or nothing but gymnastics. There is no reason to believe that the schools received any subvention from the State;†

\* Morals, i. p. 9 (Goodwin). Cp. Plato, Alc. i. p. 122 B. σοὶ δέ, ὦ 'Αλκ. Περικλῆς ἐπέστησ παιδαγωγὸν τῶν οἰκετῶν τὸν ἀχρειότατον ὑπὸ γήρως; and Lysis, ad fin., where the pedagogues appear as very boorish. Ussing notices that where they are represented on monuments they have barbaric features and dress (p. 67). Cp. Stark's Niobe u. Niobiden, Pl. ii. iv. vii. xvi. xix.

† Cp. [Plato] Alcib. i. p. 122 B. τῆς δὲ σῆς γενέσεως, ὦ

Cp. Laws, p. 794 and Ar. Pol. iv. (vii.), 17. I follow here Hermann in Charikles, ii. 23, rather than Schömann, Gr. Alt. i. 519.

they appear to have been without exception "private venture" schools, and, as might have been expected, of very various degrees of merit. Demosthenes, when taunting Aeschines with the lowness of his origin, speaks of the school kept by the father of the latter in terms of great contempt: διδάσκων γράμματα, ὡς ἐγὼ τῶν πρεσβυτέρων ἀκούω, πρὸς τῷ τοῦ Ἥρω τοῦ ἰατροῦ, ὅπως ἐδύνατο, ἀλλ' οὖν ἐν ταύτῃ γε ἔζη. But in the speech *de Corona* he claims for himself that when he was a boy he went to suitable schools. What the customary fees were we have no means of knowing; for the charges of rhetoricians and sophists —which are frequently mentioned—give us no clue to the practice in ordinary day-schools.\* But though they were not supported by the State, they were subject to a rigorous official supervision, at least, so far as the character of the teachers and the regulations of the school were concerned.

Ἀλκιβιάδη, καὶ τροφῆς, καὶ παιδείας, ἢ ἄλλου ὁτουοῦν Ἀθηναίων, ὡς ἔπος εἰπεῖν, οὐδενὶ μέλει.

\* Dem. F. L. p. 419 (p. 158 ed. Shilleto). Cp. de Cor. p. 313, where we have some curious details on the "interior" of a school at Athens. From Ar. Nub. 965, it is evident that they were spread over the various districts (κῶμαι) of the city.

Aeschines (in Timarch. §§ 9, 10) says: "The lawgiver shows a certain distrust of the teachers, to whom of necessity we commit our children, though their livelihood depends upon their character for morality, and the loss of this would reduce them to beggary; for he explicitly ordains in the first place the hour at which a free-born boy is to come to the school, and secondly the number of boys with whom he is to be taught, and when he is to leave; and he forbids teachers to open their schools, or trainers their wrestling-grounds, before sunrise, and orders them to close them before sunset, feeling the greatest distrust of solitude and darkness; and he ordains who are to be the boys who frequent these schools, and what is to be their age, and what magistrate is to superintend them."\* But we have no means of knowing to what magistrate this duty was allotted. We find at Athens no παιδονόμοι, such as existed in

---

\* Some additional details are added by the laws quoted in § 12, but their genuineness, as is the case with most of those quoted by the orators, is open to the gravest suspicion. Cp. Franke's edition and K. F. Hermann in Charikles, ii. p. 21.

Sparta and elsewhere; and though in later times we have mention of σωφρονισταί, κοσμηταί and ὑποκοσμηταί, who exercised a control over the gymnasia, these seem to belong entirely to the period when Athens had become the University of the Roman Empire, and its schools were thronged by students from every province.* To such schools, then, did the Athenian boys resort from an early age to be taught the limited curriculum which was then regarded as furnishing the needful training for a citizen. It is noteworthy that we find in Athens

*Aims of education.*

---

\* Cp. Schömann Griech. Alterth. i. p. 525. Of the ἐπιμεληταὶ τῶν ἐφήβων mentioned by Dinarchus (Hermann Pol. Ant. § 150, 4), we know next to nothing; the allusion in Dem. Fals. Leg. p. 433, is very vague, and need not refer to any special magistracy (cp. however Böckh, Public Economy, book ii. c. xvi.); and the genuineness of Plato's Axiochus is much too doubtful to allow us to argue anything from the expressions in p. 367 A. On the University character of Athens at a later time cp. Dr. Newman's Historical Sketches, cc. iii. iv. vi. vii., and especially Neubauer's *Commentationes Epigraphicae*, with the review by Mr. E. L. Hicks in Academy, I. 141. But that it was already beginning to assume this character is shown, not merely by phrases like κοινὸν παιδευτήριον πᾶσιν ἀνθρώποις (Diod. xiii. 27) and "Salvete Athenae, quae nutrices Graeciae" (Plaut. Stich. 649— probably preserved from the original by Menander), but also from [Æschin.] Epist. xii. 699. καὶ ἕτεροι μὲν, ὡς ἔοικε, τοὺς ἑαυτῶν παῖδας, τοὺς ἢ ἐν Βοιωτίᾳ γεννηθέντας ἢ ἐν Αἰτωλίᾳ, πρὸς ὑμᾶς πέμπουσι τῆς αὐτόθι παιδείας μεθέξοντας.

a clear comprehension of the essential character of liberal education. The deluded endeavour after "practical utility," which proves so misleading to much of the popular education of our own day, was then unknown, or known only to be branded as unworthy and contemptible. No special training was given for special needs in after life; the Athenians judged aright that the acquirements needed for particular trades or professions might safely be left to be gained at a later stage by those who intended to make use of them.* But the teaching which the nation encouraged, if it did not prescribe it, aimed at something better than the production of "commercial men;" it endeavoured to give the free and general culture becoming to a citizen of the "school of Hellas." As Aristotle says, "to be always in quest of what is useful is by no means becoming to high-minded gentlemen" (τοῖς μεγαλοψύχοις καὶ

---

\* Cp. Curtius, ii. 417, and Hermann in Charikles, ii. 32, "der Unterricht ... gerade eine Erhebung über die Banausie des alltäglichen Bedarfes bezweckte." Cp. also Wittmann, Erziehung und Unterricht bei Platon, p. 9. Hippocrates in the Protagoras says that he learnt music and gymnastics —οὐκ ἐπὶ τέχνῃ ἀλλ' ἐπὶ παιδείᾳ.

Pol. v. (viii.) 3. τοῖς ἐλευθέροις). Its subjects were limited in range, but they gained in depth and thoroughness more than they lost in extent. "The mental culture was but plain and simple, yet it took hold of the entire man: and this all the more deeply and energetically, inasmuch as the youthful mind was not distracted by a multiplicitous variety, and could, therefore, devote a proportionately closer devotion to the mental food, and to the materials of culture offered to it." (Curtius ii. 416.)\*

*Reading and writing.* In "music" the first stage, of course, was the study of γράμματα, which included

---

\* In the following sketch of the subjects of education, it must be remembered that they were strictly confined to boys. The education given to Athenian girls is adequately summed up in the words of Ischomachus in Xenophon's Oeconomicus, c. vii. 5. Socrates asks him whether he had himself trained (ἐπαίδευσας) his wife to be as she ought to be, or whether when he received her from her father and mother she knew how to discharge all her duties. And Ischomachus replies: καὶ τί ἂν ἐπισταμένην αὐτὴν παρέλαβον, ἣ ἔτη μὲν οὔπω πεντεκαίδεκα γεγονυῖα ἦλθε πρὸς ἐμέ, τὸν δ' ἔμπροσθεν χρόνον ἔζη ὑπὸ πολλῆς ἐπιμελείας ὅπως ἐλάχιστα μὲν ὄψοιτο, ἐλάχιστα δ' ἀκούσοιτο, ἐλάχιστα δ' ἔροιτο; "Why what could she have known, when I married her? She was not fifteen years of age when she came to me, and during the whole of the time before her marriage great pains had been taken with her that she might see as little as possible, bear as little as possible, and ask as little as possible." Then follows a very pretty sketch of the way in which he taught her various duties.

reading and writing. Whether arithmetic was added in the Athenian schools, as Plato (Laws, vii. 819) wished it to be in his ideal State, seems to Hermann more than doubtful, on the ground that a matter of merely practical value was never reckoned as παιδεία; but it is hardly likely that such an essential branch of knowledge should have been wholly passed over.* We find that the knowledge of the use of the *abacus* or calculating-board was common in daily life. With regard to reading, Becker appears to think that when the names and powers of the letters had been mastered, the pupils next began to read by the syllabic method;† but

Cp. Charikles, ii. 32.

Cp. Jebb's Theophrastus, pp. 189, 217.

---

\* Mathematics certainly were not wholly neglected, as we may see from the beginning of the Erastae (the genuineness of which Mr. Grote satisfactorily defends, i. 452), where, in the house of Dionysius the schoolmaster, two youths are represented as debating some geometrical problem. Plato gives us an idea of how he would have it taught in the well-known passage of the Meno (84 D, 85 B); and the importance which he attached to the study comes out in many of his works (cp. esp. Rep. vii. 522 E, 525 D, 528 B, Legg. v. 747 B. He uses mathematical examples *inter alios locos* in Euthyph. 12 D, Theaet. 147 D). But how far the study of mathematics was pursued at schools, and how far it was left to later life, we have no means of determining.

† If I understand aright Becker's "Syllabirmethode," as opposed to the "reine Buchstabirmethode," he denotes by the former the admirable method of learning to read

the passage quoted by him from Dionysius of Halicarnassus hardly bears out the interpretation which he puts upon it; and it is expressly contradicted by another passage quoted from Athenaeus, which tells us how there was a kind of metrical chant used in schools, running βῆτα ἄλφα βα, βῆτα εἶ βε, βῆτα ἢ βη, βῆτα ἰῶτα βι, βῆτα οὖ βο, βῆτα ὦ βω· καὶ πάλιν ἐν ἀντιστρόφῳ τοῦ μέλους καὶ τοῦ μέτρου, γάμμα ἄλφα, γάμμα εἶ κ.τ.λ. καὶ ἐπὶ τῶν λοιπῶν συλλαβῶν ὁμοίως ἑκάστων.* Writing was taught by copies, the masters drawing lines on which the pupil was to write the letters set before him, as Plato tells us (Protag. 326 D) οἱ γραμματισταὶ τοῖς μήπω δεινοῖς γράφειν τῶν παίδων ὑπογράψαντες γραμμὰς τῇ γραφίδι

*margin:* Cp. Ussing, op. cit. p. 107, note.
Athen. x. 79, p. 453.
*Writing.*

(recently brought into more general notice by Messrs. Meiklejohn and Sonnenschein), in which the pupil is not taught the *names* of the letters at first, but simply their powers, so that he is able to combine them into syllables at once, without the confusion of ideas that often arises from the common system. But this is one of the somewhat numerous passages in which the English abridgement of "Charicles" purchases brevity at the cost of the sacrifice of the most important phrases and clauses of the original.

\* In Dionys. Halic. (de admir. vi dic. in Demosth. c. 52) we have the following account of the various stages in learning to read: "First, we learn the names of the letters (στοιχεῖα τῆς φωνῆς) that is the γράμματα, then their several forms and values (τύπους καὶ δυναμεῖς), then syllables and

οὕτω τὸ γραμματεῖον διδόασι καὶ ἀναγκάζουσι γράφειν κατὰ τὴν ὑφήγησιν τῶν γραμμῶν: here γραμμαί must mean the lines drawn for the guidance of the pupil, and not, as some would understand it, letters which the pupil was to trace over; though the latter practice was also adopted, as we see from a passage in Quintilian (I. 1. 27, Halm): "Cum vero iam ductus sequi coeperit (puer), non inutile erit literas tabellae quam optime insculpi, ut per illos velut sulcos ducatur stilus" (cp. also v. 14, 31). But in the judgment of Plato (Laws, vii. 810) too much attention ought not to be given to handwriting: if boys cannot readily acquire quickness and beauty of writing in the time allowed to their studies, they must be content to let it alone. *Cp. Sauppe ad loc.*

As soon as the needful rudiments of reading and writing were mastered, the *Study of the poets.*

their modifications (τὰ περὶ ταῦτα πάθη), and finally nouns and verbs and connecting particles, and the changes which they undergo (ὀνόματα καὶ ῥήματα καὶ συνδέσμους καὶ τὰ συμβεβηκότα τούτοις, συστολὰς, ἐκτάσεις, ὀξύτητας, βαρύτητας, πτώσεις, ἀριθμούς, ἐγκλίσεις, τὰ ἄλλα παραπλήσια τούτοις). Then we begin to read and to write, at first syllable by syllable, very slowly, and then more rapidly, as we acquire some familiarity."

teachers commenced the more important part of literary education. "Placing the pupils," as Plato says, "on the benches, they make them read and learn by heart the poems of good poets, in which are many moral lessons, many tales and eulogies and lays of the brave men of old, that the boys may imitate them with emulation, and strive to become such themselves." It appears that in very early times there were selections from the works of Homer, Hesiod, Theognis, Phokylides, and many of the lyric poets, expressly intended for use in schools. Some, like Nikeratos in Xenophon's Symposium, went so far as to learn by heart the whole of the Iliad and the Odyssey; and he boasts that he could still repeat them from memory. At first, we may believe that these poems were simply explained to the boys, the meaning of words and phrases discussed, and obscure allusions interpreted.* But before long γράμματα

*Protag. 325 ε*

*Schömann Gr. Alt. i. 519. From Ar. Av. 471, it is clear that Æsop was used as an elementary book: ἀμαθὴς γὰρ ἔφυς ... οὐδ' Αἴσωπον πεπάτηκας.*

---

\* We have an example of the kind of catechising that was practised in the fragments of the Δαιταλεῖς of Aristophanes, quoted by Galen in the preface to the Lexicon Hippocraticum; *e.g.*—

was supplemented by the other great section of μουσική; and the boys were taught to chant the poems they had learnt to a suitable accompaniment on the lyre. According to Plato κιθάρισις was not to commence till the boys were thirteen years of age, when they had already spent three years on the study of letters; but we have no means, I believe, of determining whether in laying down this regulation for his ideal State, he was following or correcting the practice common at Athens. It is evident, of course, that a certain time would have to be spent in acquiring a command over the instrument *

*Music.*

Laws, vii. p. 810 A.

πρὸς ταῦτα σὺ λέξον Ὁμηρείους γλώττας, τί καλοῦσι κόρυμβα.
and again—
ὁ μὲν οὖν σός, ἐμὸς δ' οὗτος ἀδελφὸς φρασάτω τί καλοῦσιν ἰδυίους.

Cp. Aristophanis Fragmenta, ed. Dindorf. (1869) p. 182. The Δαιταλεῖς would have probably furnished us with many more hints on Athenian education, had it been preserved to us; for the subject appears to have been furnished by two brothers, one addicted to the old-fashioned methods of learning, another to new-fangled ways, regarded of course with no little disfavour by Aristophanes.

* Hermann notices that the λύρα is more frequently mentioned by the earlier writers (with the exception of Homer, where the word does not occur) than the κίθαρα; but the latter was a much lighter instrument (Dict. Ant. s.v. Lyra), and was therefore probably used in schools. The use of the flute, so common in Boeotia, was at one time prac-

Charikles, ii. 38.

*Influence of music.*

Vol. i. pp. 132-3 (Goodwin).

before it could be employed to accompany the voice in recitations or chantings. We have already noticed (p. 35) the importance attached to the study of music. Plutarch in his treatise on the subject is only expressing the common Greek sentiment when he writes: "Whoever he be that shall give his mind to the study of music in his youth, if he meet with a musical education proper for the forming and regulating his inclinations, he will be sure to applaud and embrace that which is noble and generous, and to rebuke and blame the contrary, as well in other things as in what belongs to music. And by that means he will become clear from all reproachful actions, for now having reaped the noblest fruit of music, he may be of great use, not only to himself, but to the commonwealth; while music teaches him to abstain from everything that is indecent, both in word and deed, and to observe

tised at Athens, but it was afterwards discouraged, partly because its music was supposed to be too passionate and orgiastic in its character, and partly because it could not be accompanied by the voice of the performer. Cp. Arist. Pol. v. (viii.) 6, 6, and Cic. pro Mur. 13, 29.

decorum, temperance, and regularity" (§ 41). And again yet more emphatically, (§ 31): "The right moulding or ruin of ingenuous manners and civil conduct lies in a well-grounded musical education." Plato constantly expresses similar opinions, as, for instance, in the Timaeus (p. 47 D), where he says that "harmony is not regarded by him who intelligently uses the Muses as given by them with a view to irrational pleasure, but with a view to the inharmonical course of the soul and as an ally for the purpose of reducing this into harmony and agreement with itself; and rhythm was given by them for the same purpose, on account of the irregular and graceless ways which prevail among mankind generally, and to help us against them." And again in the Protagoras (p. 326 B.): "They make rhythm and harmony familiar to the souls of boys, that they may grow more gentle, and graceful, and harmonious, and so be of service both in words and deeds; for the whole life of man stands in need of grace and harmony." Hence we find Cp. too Rep. iii. 401; Laws, vii. 812; and Arist. Pol. v. (viii.) 5, 15-25.

that the greatest care was taken to adapt the tunes to the poems to which they were to be sung, and to provide that both the one and the other should be pure, noble, and elevating. It is quite as much on ethical as on æsthetic grounds that Aristophanes attacks so fiercely the corrupters of the music of his own day. Philoxenus, Kinesias, and Phrynis all come in for his censures, as contributing, by their effeminate and enervating music, to the degeneracy of the Athenian youth. And in the controversy between Aeschylus and Euripides in the Ranae, as to their respective merits, hardly less importance is attached to the formal (*i.e.* the rhythmical and musical) side of their works than to the material or moral and religious side. Mr. Grote has pointed out how even a practical politician like Polybius considers a training in music indispensable for the softening of violent and sanguinary tempers. The Athenian critics found the main object of their attacks in the later developements of the Dithyramb, which had always been allowed

*Cp. Nub. 971.*

*Plato, iii. 336.*

*Polyb. iv. pp. 20. 21, of the rude Arcadians of Kynaetha.*

great laxity of construction, but which, towards the close of the fifth century before Christ, in the hands of Melanippides, Philoxenus, Kinesias, Phrynis, Timotheus, and Polyeidus went through a gradual process of degradation. The principal ground of censure with the philosophers and moralists was that which Plato (Gorg. 501 D) expressly adduces in the case of Kinesias, that the musicians had come to attach no importance to making their hearers better, and only sought to please the greater number. Hence, as we shall shortly see, Plato and Aristotle, in their ideal schemes of national education, insist repeatedly on the necessity of a rigid official control of the music taught to the young, that it may not fail to secure the elevating results which it is capable of producing.*

---

\* The *moral* part of the education given in an Athenian school, so far as it concerned propriety of behaviour rather than justness of views, or temperance and courage of spirit, was summed up under the name εὐκοσμία. To this Plato in the Protagoras attaches much importance, and even says (speaking under the person of Protagoras), εἰς διδασκάλων πέμποντες [οἱ πατέρες] πολὺ μᾶλλον ἐντέλλονται ἐπιμελεῖσθαι εὐκοσμίας τῶν παίδων ἢ γραμμάτων τε καὶ κιθαρίσεως (p. 325 D). A graphic sketch of the points which were con-

In the earlier days of the Athenian State, the education of a boy was considered complete when he had acquired

sidered essential to ἐυκοσμία is given in the *locus classicus* on Athenian education in Aristoph. Nub. 961-983. From this it appears that a modest silence, a reserved behaviour in the streets, a decent position in sitting, and an absence of greediness at meals, were regarded as distinguishing features of a well-trained boy.

It is probable that both branches of μουσική, letters and music, were often taught by the same master (Cp. Ar. Eq. 181, with Kock's note); but for gymnastics, as we see from the passage in the Clouds, boys went to a different master, the παιδοτρίβης. Cramer (Geschichte der Erziehung, i. 287) regards this profession as one peculiar to Athens; but he assigns no authority, nor is such a limitation probable from the nature of the case. As compared with Sparta, where the physical training of the youth of the nation was conducted wholly by State officials, it is certain that private teachers of gymnastics were far more numerous at Athens; but all our evidence goes to show that they were common in every town of Greece. Whether there was any difference between the παιδοτρίβης and the γυμναστής is not clear: from the words of Aristotle (παραδοτέον τοὺς παῖδας γυμναστικῇ καὶ παιδοτριβικῇ· τούτων γὰρ ἡ μὲν ποιάν τινα ποιεῖ τὴν ἕξιν τοῦ σώματος ἡ δὲ τὰ ἔργα—Pol. v. [viii.] 3, 2) it seems that the one was especially concerned with the general health and vigour of his pupils, the other with their skill and agility in the performance of gymnastic feats. But the terms are often interchanged. Still after the very careful discussion by Becker and Hermann (Charikles, ii. 185-194) it seems probable that the gymnasium was especially devoted to the amusement of men, the palaestra to the training of boys. [Mr. Jebb, in his charming edition of Theophrastus (p. 237), makes the distinction to consist rather in the fact that the palaestra was strictly only a school for boxing and wrestling, while the gymnasium properly meant a place of more general resort and more various resources, including

# THE SOPHISTS.

the elements of gymnastics and of music.*
Naturally, the process of training was
continued longer in some cases than in
others. In a passage already quoted Plato
tells us, what we might have argued
from analogy, that the sons of wealthier
citizens remained at school longer than
those of the poorer ones; and probably
some of them continued their studies
until the time for their solemn admission
into the ranks of the περίπολοι, when they
were enrolled, each in his own deme,
presented with a shield and spear in the
theatre before the assembled people, and

---

grounds for running and archery, javelin-ranges, baths, &c.]
It would lead us too far from the present subject to enter
upon a consideration of the particular exercises practised in
the palaestra. There is a very graphic description of these
in the Anacharsis of Lucian; and the whole question is
exhaustively discussed by Hermann, Privatalt. pp. 296–304.
And it is happily needless to dwell upon the serious moral
evils that attended upon them so often—

Non ragionam di lor, ma guarda e passa.

* Aristotle tells us (Pol. v. (viii.) 2) that to the three main
branches of education, letters, gymnastics, and music, some
added a fourth—drawing. According to Plin. H.N. xxxv.
17, this was owing to the influence of Pamphilus of Sicyon
(Flor. B.C. 390–350) : Pamphili auctoritate effectum est
Sicyone primum, deinde in tota Graecia ut pueri ingenui
omnes artem graphicen hoc est picturam in buxo docerentur,
recipereturque ars ea in primum gradum artium liberalium.

required to take an oath of obedience to the laws and devotion to the State. Perhaps the more elaborate training in the use of arms, in the art of war, and in the elements of drawing, which we find mentioned by Plato and Aristotle, was already known. But it is with the appearance of the Sophists that we have the first intimations of anything like a regular system of higher education. This is not the place for any attempt at a full discussion of the character and work of that remarkable class of men. Since the appearance of Mr. Grote's justly famous chapter on the subject, the question has been so thoroughly discussed, from every point of view, by Mr. Cope, Mr. Lewes, Dr. Schömann, Dr. Zeller, Sir A. Grant, Professor Campbell, Professor Jowett, and Mr. Henry Sidgwick, that nothing less than an essay devoted to the purpose would be sufficient to state and examine the various arguments that have been adduced. I must be content here to express my full concurrence in the words of Mr. Sidgwick, that Grote's account "has the merit of a

*Cp. Schömann, Alterth. i. 372, where the words of the oath are given.*

*The Sophists.*

*Journal of Philology, vol. iv. p. 288.*

historical discovery of the highest order," and that "the main substance of his conclusions is as clear and certain as anything of the kind can possibly be." The general purport of his views I take to be somewhat as follows: that towards the middle of the fifth century before Christ, various teachers appeared in different parts of Greece, most of whom were, at some time of their life, attracted to Athens as the centre of the highest Hellenic life; that they judged the traditional system of education to be imperfect in many ways, and capable of being supplemented by instruction of considerable value for practical life; that this instruction they professed themselves able to give, and willing to give for money; that in doing so some of their number took up with superficial and dangerous views of truth which drew upon them the unsparing hostility of men like Sokrates and Plato, while the way in which they ran counter to popular prejudices, and above all the fact that they received pay for their teaching, exposed them to the ill-will of the uneducated; but

*Their character and influence.*

that it is equally erroneous to regard them as a sect with any common agreement as to doctrines, and as consciously and without exception teaching immorality. It cannot be denied, I think, that their method of investigation was as a rule deficient in depth and thoroughness; that it was often dangerous; that it contributed something to the decay of morality at Athens, and would have contributed more if it had not been for the resolute opposition of the Socratic schools; and that Plato was fully justified in much, if not all, his polemics against their prevailing tendencies. Nor, on the other hand, can we doubt their services to the developement of the higher education of the time. It would not have been a little if the bold speculations of some of their number on ethics and politics had done nothing more than call up the more thorough and far-reaching discussions of Plato and Aristotle. There is a very real sense in which men like Protagoras, Prodikus, and even Gorgias and Hippias, are to be called the fathers of moral philosophy rather than Sokrates.

*Their influence not wholly for evil.*

It was not he who called down philosophy from the heights to dwell among men; but finding her already directed by the Sophists to the business of the agora and the home, he guided her by his shrewd common-sense and unfailing devotion to righteousness to the method whereby she might deal with it aright. The step from the era of "unconscious morality" (*Sittlichkeit*, as the Germans call it) to that of philosophical morality (*Moralität*), when moral precepts rest no longer upon tradition, but upon "a system of reasoned truth," must, of necessity, be accompanied by much shaking of accepted beliefs, by much scepticism, unreasonable as well as reasonable; but for all that the step is imperatively needful for the progress of the race. Traditional morality is secure only so long as it is unimpugned; at the first assault with the weapons of reason, it must furnish itself with arms of the same temper and forging, if it is to hold its own. It is probable, nay almost certain, that Plato exaggerates the shameless audacity of men like Thra-

<sup>Cp. Stirling. Notes to Schwegler, p. 395.</sup>

<sup>Grote's Plato, i. vi.</sup>

symachus and Polus; yet it cannot be doubted that the Gorgias and the Republic, and we may even add the Nicomachean Ethics and the Politics, are the immediate outcome of the speculations first set on foot by the Sophists. But their contributions to the advance of knowledge were not wholly indirect. The importance which was commonly assigned to dialectic and rhetoric naturally led to a closer study of the nature of words and sentences; and hence we find the beginnings of the science of grammar attributed to some of the leading Sophists. Protagoras was the first to discuss the gender of substantives, the tenses (μέρη χρόνων) and the modality of propositions,* and generally the correctness of diction (ὀρθοέπεια— Plat. Phaedr. 267 C). Prodikus—as we learn from Plato's delicious parodies—

*The study of grammar.*

---

* Cp. Zeller, Philosophie der Griechen, i. 787 : "Protagoras und Prodikus—die ersten Begründer einer wissenschaftlichen Sprachforschung bei den Griechen geworden sind." It is commonly said that he discussed the *moods*, and Zeller (u.s. note 5) defends this view; but Spengel (Συναγωγὴ τεχνῶν, p. 44) and Benfey—Geschichte der Sprachwissenschaft (p. 111)—have, I think, clearly disproved it.

## THE SOPHISTS.

taught the distinctions between synonymous terms, not without a certain over-refinement and conscious affectation. Hippias laid down rules for correctness in language generally, but especially with reference to rhythm, and to the powers of the several letters (γραμμάτων δυνάμεις). And there was hardly one of the more prominent Sophists who did not leave behind him a treatise on rhetoric (τέχνη). The fragments of these have been collected in an early work of Leonard Spengel's, Συναγωγὴ τεχνῶν. So deeply did the new studies strike root into the higher Athenian education, that Antisthenes, who was at once a pupil of Sokrates and of Gorgias, says ἀρχὴ παιδεύσεως ἡ τῶν ὀνομάτων ἐπίσκεψις;* and the earnestness with which the Platonic Sokrates repeatedly utters his warnings against the

Cp. Benfey, Geschichte, p. 112.

---

\* At the same time we have abundant proof of the general ignorance of grammar in the fact that Plato again and again introduces its elementary conceptions as novelties to his hearers. Cp. Phileb. 18 B; Cratyl. 424 C; Theaet. 203 B; and see especially the curious difficulty with which the very intelligent Theaetetus follows the grammatical illustrations of the Elean in Sophistes, pp. 261-262. Cp. Wittmann, Erziehung und Unterricht bei Platon. p. 22, and Grote's Plato, ii. 434.

danger of deriving a knowledge of things solely from their names, is a sufficient proof of the great influence of the Sophistic methods. If further evidence were wanted, it would be supplied by the jests of Aristophanes (Nub. 662, 599) and by the fact that the comic poet Kallias wrote a Γραμματικὴ Τραγῳδία on purpose to turn them into ridicule.* Of the interest which the presence of one of the famous Sophists caused at Athens we have a well-known and extremely graphic description at the beginning of Plato's Protagoras. It is plain that as early as the time of the Peloponnesian war a new element had been introduced into Athenian education, which for nearly a thousand

*The higher learning.*

---

* Cramer, on the other hand (Geschichte der Erziehung, ii. p. 212), considers that the object of Kallias was rather to encourage the introduction of the new Ionian alphabet, which, in 403, was officially substituted for the old Cadmean alphabet of sixteen letters; and that he endeavoured to give to grammatical rules a certain attractiveness by throwing them into the form of verse. I have not had an opportunity of consulting Welcker's paper "Das ABC-buch des Kallias in Form einer Tragödie," in the Rhein. Museum, I. i. 137, &c. But Kallias is certainly best known as a comic poet. Dr. Schmitz, however (in Dict. Biog. I. v.), considers it doubtful whether the comic poet is to be identified with the writer of the Γραμματικὴ Τραγῳδία.

years was never to be wanting to it. Not recognised by the Government—at least till a later date—and owing their attraction solely to their reputation for superior learning or ability, the long series of Sophists, rhetoricians, and philosophers continued to give that instruction in the higher learning which, found nowhere else in equal fulness, was destined to keep alive, far into the Christian centuries, the fame of Athens as the university of the civilised world. The general nature, tendency, and results of their teaching would furnish a theme of the highest interest. For, indeed, it would be little less than the history of the completest culture given to the human intellect during a period of surpassing importance. It would comprise all the most hopeful, sober, resolute, and finally despairing attempts of human philosophy to solve for itself the mysteries of life and death, of man and of the world around him, before the "dayspring from on high" visited us, and the "Sun of Righteousness" arose with healing in His wings on a weary, sin-sick earth. But the theme would lead us far away from our present subject, and, indeed, it would need no little courage to attempt it. We must simply take notice of the fact that above and beyond the training of the palaestra and the school, there was an education open to every free-born Athenian youth, which, for the untrammelled play which it gave to the highest powers of reason and fancy on the most important themes, for the keen rivalry of opposing schools, for the acuteness, and in many cases the moral earnestness, of the teachers, for the free intercourse which it promoted among students from every part of the Hellenic world, has been rarely if ever equalled. The early training of the Athenian boys in grammar and music (as the words were at that time understood), developed a refinement of taste which became instinctive; the close and constant study of the poets of their country filled their minds with noble thoughts and beautiful fancies; and the assiduous practice of gymnastics shaped and moulded frames of manly grace and vigour. But that which made the Athenian intellect what it was, which lent it its unrivalled suppleness, and created its unfailing versatility, was not so much the formal training of boyhood, as the daily intercourse of the youthful citizen with acute and disciplined philosophers.

Again, we should fail to take account of a most important element in Athenian education if we passed over wholly in silence the results upon the younger men of the richness of the common national life. When critics like Johnson sneered at the Athenians as ignorant barbarians, he was not answered by enumerating the schools that abounded in Athens, and culling from ancient writers references to the extent and completeness of the training in grammar and rhetoric. But he was reminded that "to be a citizen was to be a legislator—a soldier—a judge,—one upon whose voice might depend the fate of the wealthiest tributary state, of the most important public man."* An Athenian's

*Influence of the national life.*

* Cp. Macaulay's "Essay on the Athenian Orators," and

books were few, but those which he had were the writings of the poets whom the consentient voices of all later civilisation have pronounced to be unrivalled models. And they were known with a thoroughness which outweighed a thousandfold in its value for mental discipline the hasty skimming of innumerable newspapers and pamphlets. But above all things the Athenian of the age of Perikles was living in an atmosphere of unequalled genius and culture. He took his way past the temples where the friezes of Phidias seemed to breathe and struggle, under the shadow of the colonnades reared by the craft of Iktinus or Kallikrates and glowing with the hues of Polygnotus, to the agora where, like his Aryan forefathers by the shores of the Caspian, or his Teutonic cousins in the forests of Germany, he was to take his part as a free man in fixing the fortunes of his country. There he would listen,

Curtius Hist. ii. 415: "A constitution founded in a spirit of sublime wisdom, and having in view the participation of the whole civic community in public life, necessarily and of itself became, in the fullest sense of the word, a public discipline."

with the eagerness of one who knew that all he held most dear was trembling in the balance, to the pregnant eloquence of Perikles. Or, in later times, he would measure the sober prudence of Nikias against the boisterous turbulence of Kleon, or the daring brilliance of Alkibiades. Then, as the Great Dionysia came round once more with the spring-time, and the sea was open again for traffic, and from every quarter of Hellas the strangers flocked for pleasure or business, he would take his place betimes in the theatre of Dionysius, and gaze from sunrise to sunset on the successive tragedies in which Sophokles, and Euripides, and Ion of Chios, were contending for the prize of poetry. Or, at the lesser festivals, he would listen to the wonderful comedies of Eupolis, Aristophanes, or the old Kratinus, with their rollicking fun and snatches of sweetest melody, their savage attacks on personal enemies and merry jeers at well-known cowards or wantons, and, underlying all, their weighty allusions and earnest political purpose. As he passed through the

*Cp. Becker's Charikles, i. scene x.*

market-place, or looked in at one of the wrestling schools, he may have chanced to come upon a group of men in eager conversation, or hanging with breathless interest on the words of one of their number; and he may have found himself listening to an harangue of Gorgias, or to a fragment of the unsparing dialectic of Sokrates. What could books do more for a man who was receiving an education such as this? "It was what the student gazed on, what he heard, what he caught by the magic of sympathy, not what he read, which was the education furnished by Athens." Not by her *discipline*, like Sparta and Rome, but by the unfailing charm of her gracious *influence*, did Athens train her children. The writer whose words have just been quoted, has summarized, with all his wonted perfection of diction, the famous passage in the funeral speech of Perikles, and his language may fitly express the better side of that ideal of life to which Athenian education was directed: "While in private and personal matters, each Athenian was suffered to please himself, without

[margin: J. H. Newman, Historical Sketches, p. 40.]

[margin: *Character of Athenian life.*]

any tyrannous public opinion to make him feel uncomfortable, the same freedom of will did but unite the people, one and all, in concerns of national interest, because obedience to the magistrates and the laws was with them a sort of passion, to shrink from dishonour an instinct, and to repress injustice an indulgence. They could be splendid in their feasts and festivals without extravagance, because the crowds whom they attracted from abroad repaid them for the outlay; and such large hospitality did but cherish in them a frank, unsuspicious and courageous spirit, which better protected them than a pile of state secrets and exclusive laws. Nor did this joyous mode of life relax them as it might relax a less noble race; for they were warlike without effort and expert without training, and rich in resource by the gift of nature, and after their fill of pleasure they were only more gallant in the field, and more patient and enduring on the march. They cultivated the fine arts with too much taste to be expensive, and they studied the sciences with too much point to be effeminate: debate did not blunt their energy, nor foresight of danger chill their daring: but as their tragic poet expresses it, 'the loves were the attendants upon wisdom, and had a share in the acts of every virtue.'" It is needless to say that there is another side to the picture. A purely *laissez-faire* policy in education is not likely to be wholly successful, even under the most favouring circumstances; and there are darker shades to be added to the painting, before we can accept it as a just delineation. The attraction of influence tells, as nothing else will, with those who are nobly-minded; and the unfettered "Lern- und Lehr-Freiheit," which has long been the boast of Germany, and to which our own English universities are happily making some approaches, is capable of producing results more valuable than any which discipline can attain to. But for the mass of men something more is needed than the simple charms of knowledge and virtue to constrain them to the steady and strenuous

*Margin notes:* Newman, Historical Sketches, pp. 83–84. — *Influence and discipline compared.*

pursuit which is needful to achieve success. We may well believe that, as Spartan apologists were compelled to admit, a good Athenian was a better man than the best of Spartans. And yet we may see that many a young Athenian citizen would have been far better for something of the stern control which marked the discipline of Lacedaemon. The evils that arose as freedom degenerated into license were felt all the more deeply in a city where the only guard of the laws was the tone of public opinion. All that a genuine lover of the free Attic life, like Curtius, can venture to say is that "the old Attic culture which had proved its worth during the troubles of the Persian wars, the ancient morality and piety, had retained their dominion as late as the days of Pericles, even without the binding force of laws such as held sway at Sparta."* In the time of Plato and Aristotle the danger of the Athenian tendency to indivi-

* The repeated attacks of Aristophanes on the corruption of the youth of his own time are of course exaggerations; but they cannot have been without a very considerable basis of reality.

*The Stoics and the Epicureans foreshadowed.*

dual freedom of thought and action, had clearly presented itself to the view of every thinker: and hence we shall find them tending rather towards the institutions of her rival. We may see perhaps in the educational systems of Athens and Sparta respectively some foreshadowing of the two great schools of philosophy that were afterwards to divide between them so large a portion of the Hellenic and Roman world. Athens appears to have learnt beforehand the philosophy of Epicurus—the identity of goodness with beauty and joy—and the strength and the weakness of Epicureanism were hers. We find on the one hand the winning grace of life, the genial ease, the kindly brightness which lend so much attraction to the figures of Epicurus himself and the best of his followers— we need refer only to Vergil and Horace; but on the other hand we have a license that readily degenerates into licentiousness, an indulgence of the purer impulses of the heart that too soon passes into an indulgence of each and all. The identification of virtue with happiness leads very quickly to the identification of pleasure with virtue; the love of the Beautiful becomes the love of the Sensual; and the pursuit of that which is most alluring lasts, even when goodness has lost her power to be held as such. Sparta, on the other hand, tended towards that rigid suppression of natural desires, and that absolute submission to external law, which formed the strength of Stoicism, just as their exaggeration proved in the long run its fatal weakness. There were many, undoubtedly, to whom the rigid discipline of Sparta, or the severe asceticism of the Porch, was safer than a freer and a more genial system; but as on the one hand the virtue that was the product of Law fell short of the goodness that sprang from a love of the ideal Good,* so, on the other, the attempt to impose on all mankind a burden greater than they could bear of necessity led to a fierce reaction, which broke the bonds of every law.

* It is needless to say that men like Epictetus and Marcus Aurelius cannot be considered as Stoics proper. Though nominally followers of Zeno and Cleanthes, they are really Eclectics in the most attractive part of their philosophy.

The evils of license are great, but it may be fairly doubted whether they are not less in magnitude and permanence than those which result from unnatural and tyrannous restrictions. The rule of Sparta was shorter and far more brutal than that of Athens; her fall was greater, her ruin more utter and irretrievable.

# CHAPTER III.

## PLATO ON NATIONAL EDUCATION.

We have now completed our survey of the popular theories of education in the two great typical Greek communities, and of the manner in which they were carried into practice; it remains that we should consider more in detail the views of the leading Athenian thinkers of the century with which we are especially dealing.

Xenophon need not long delay us. It is true that his Kyropaedia, if not actually written, as some authorities inform us, in opposition to the Republic of Plato, has this much in common with that great work, that the writer endeavours to set forth (in this case under the transparent disguise of a historical fiction) his views on the ideal constitution and government of a State.

*Xenophon's limited views.*

But the paternal despotism of a wise and virtuous prince, and not the rule of a highly cultivated body of philosophers, was the government which commended itself to the judgment of the gallant but somewhat narrow-minded mercenary; and the Persian laws, which he regards with so much approval, aim only at rearing skilful, brave, temperate, and above all obedient, soldiers. Of any higher education than that which is needful for the production of useful tools in war, there is hardly a trace to be found. The training of the intellect was limited to the cultivation of a certain power of explaining the grounds of action (Kyrop. i. 4, 3). The Persians are not supposed to know their letters, to hear or recite any poetry, or even to learn the use of any musical instrument. And Heeren has shown that even this meagre training was intended only for the members of an exclusive caste. None were to be admitted to it but those who were placed by circumstances beyond the necessity of working for their daily bread. It is needless to point out the want of analytical and specu-

*Ideen, &c., ii. 437.*

lative power, and the inferior knowledge of human nature, which make this treatise hardly deserving of mention by the side of the master-works of the Lyceum and the Academy.

Plato and Aristotle both attached the greatest importance to education, and dwelt upon it at considerable length. With both, the establishment of a perfect commonwealth was regarded as the ultimate object of all the speculations of philosophy; inasmuch as it was only in the midst of the favourable conditions afforded by a perfect State that the complete happiness and virtue of the individual could be realised. But the first requisite for the perfection of the State is a well-ordered system of education. And so Aristotle, after discussing in the Nicomachean Ethics the supreme good of the individual, and the laws of his highest excellence, proceeds in his Politics to sketch out his conception of an ideal State.* As usual with him, a certain amount of attention is given first to a purely

*Marginal notes:* Importance of education with Plato and Aristotle. Aristotle's method.

---

\* That it is an *ideal* State has been shown, against objectors, by Zeller, ii. 2, 570.

negative criticism of previous attempts in the same direction; but he proceeds only a very little way in the constructive portion of his work before he takes up the question of education, and assigns nearly a book and a half to its consideration, although his treatment of the subject is evidently fragmentary.* And Plato's matured and systematic expression of his views on education is thrown into the same form in his Republic and Laws. These two great works differ so considerably in style, in power, and in many points of detail, that some have been tempted to deny the genuineness of the latter. But after the defence of the Laws by Stallbaum, Grote, and Jowett, and the recantation by Zeller of his former extremely able attack, we may fairly consider all doubts removed. The important discrepancies seem to be fully accounted for by the different conditions under which the dialogues were written, and the different objects which they had in view. In the

*The Republic and the Laws.*

Cp. his Platonische Studien, 1-131, with his Geschichte, ii. 1, 348, 615, 641.

* It will be seen that I follow the rearrangement of the books of the Politics adopted by St. Hilaire and Congreve. Cp. Zeller, ii. 2, 523.

Republic, undoubtedly a work of Plato's prime, the philosopher endeavours, with little or no regard to the possibilities of actual life, to draw out a scheme of that polity, which should be ideally favourable to the developement of virtue, and therefore of happiness. The Laws we may with equal certainty pronounce to be the product of his extreme old age. He no longer aims at that which is the best conceivable;\* but he draws out a system of legislation for a colony which he supposes it is intended to found in a certain place in Crete. There is not only a striking failure of artistic power in the later treatise, a senile garrulity and discursiveness, a marked deficiency in the infinite grace, humour, and dramatic skill that illuminate his earlier writings, but there is also a hard and bitter tone, and above all a narrow dogmatism strangely unlike his former joyous confidence in the healthful results of the free play of reason in dialectics. It will, therefore, be needful

---

\* Strictly speaking, even the Republic does not give what Plato considered *absolutely* best; *e.g.* communism is limited to the Guardians, instead of being extended to the whole community. Cp. Grote's Plato, iii. 207 and note.

for us in many cases to distinguish the theories of the Laws from those of the Republic; and not to speak hastily of any views as held by Plato, unless at the same time we determine to what portion of his life and to what stage in his thought we are to assign them.

*The Republic.* It has been often said that the Republic is essentially a treatise on education, and Mr. Maurice characteristically objects to any such limited definition of it. Anc. Phil. p. 163 (ed. 4). the statement has much truth in it. But it needs one very important qualification. All that has been said above of the limited sense in which we can speak of a national education in Greece is true, in a still higher degree, of the conception of it held by Plato. Dividing the citizens of his ideal state into Rulers, or Guardians, Auxiliaries, and Commons, he provides a very careful and thorough education for the first class, and a rigorous training, up to a certain point, for the second, but the third, which will naturally be by far the largest, he leaves wholly without provision. It is true that Cp. Grote's Plato, iii. 212. he does not exclude them from membership of the State, as Aristotle does; on the contrary, the laborious and self-denying training of the Guardians is mainly intended to secure the happiness of the Commons, and the chief enjoyment which the former have to expect is the consciousness of doing their duty. Still the education sketched out in the Republic is the education of a small class, and the Demos is in this respect wholly neglected. It is one of the most curious points about the Republic that Plato passes over almost wholly in silence the condition of what after all he must have considered would have formed the great majority of the citizens.

We have noticed before (p. 53) the great attraction which the Spartan institutions seem to have had for Plato. He is entirely at one with them on the absolute control which the State is to exercise over the training and the manner of life of every citizen. And yet, as Mr. Grote has acutely noticed, it is rather the Athenian type of character which he aims at producing, and the common Athenian instruments of education which he approves. The excessive devotion of the Spartans to gymnastics, and their neglect of music in its wider

*The extent of his admiration for Sparta.*

Cp. Jowett's Plato, ii. 137.

Cp. Grote, Plato, iii. 175, 178.

sense, he censures as likely to make men good warriors, but not good citizens. A man who gives himself up unduly to gymnastics, "ends by becoming a hater of philosophy, uncultivated, never using the weapon of persuasion; he is like a wild beast, all violence and fierceness, and knows no other way of dealing; and he lives in all ignorance and evil conditions, and has no sense of propriety or grace." On the other hand, if he devotes himself too much to music, he is apt to become "melted and softened beyond what is good for him;" "the passion of his soul is melted out of him, and what may be called the nerves of his soul are cut away, and he becomes but a feeble warrior;" he may even grow irritable, violent, and very discontented. Therefore it is necessary that throughout life these two means of education should be kept in due proportion to each other, so that each side of the nature of man may be fitly trained and developed.

*Repub. iii. 411 (Jowett).*

*The birth and rearing of children.*  With Plato, as with Lycurgus, the care of the children of the State begins before their birth. Rigid rules are laid down for the regulation of marriage. The limits of age within which marriage for the purpose of procreation is allowed are strictly fixed; and the care which was taken at Sparta that the most suitable partners should be brought together is carried to an extreme, which has always been regarded as one of the most impracticable and repulsive features of the Republic. As Mr. Jowett justly says: "Human nature is reduced as nearly as possible to the level of the animals.... All that world of poetry and fancy which the passion of love has called forth in modern literature and romance would have been banished by Plato.... We start back horrified from this Platonic ideal, in the belief, first, that the instincts of human nature are far too strong to be crushed out in this way; secondly, that if the plan could be carried out, we should be poorly recompensed by improvements in the breed for the loss of the best things in life. The greatest regard for the least and meanest things of humanity—the deformed infant, the culprit, the insane, the idiot—truly seems to us one of the noblest results of Christianity." And yet we are bound to recognise in Plato's conception of a State regulation of marriage, involving as it does the degrading notion of a general community of wives, an honest and earnest attempt to struggle against some of the greatest and most widespread hindrances to the establishment of national well-being. It cannot be denied that there are few sources of vice and crime so fatally prolific as the manifold evils that result from improvident and ill-adjusted marriages. What the most thoughtful and far-seeing of the modern reformers of society are endeavouring to secure by the creation of habits of self-control aided by an enlightened public opinion, Plato attempted to grasp at once by a violent subversion of the foundations of human society as at present constituted. We, who are learning in medicine to trust to the restorative power of nature, and are taught by our ablest surgeons to give up the cautery and the knife for the healing magic of rest, are not likely to sympathise with "heroic remedies." And yet we may appreciate the magnitude of the evils

*Marginal notes:* Plato, ii. 145.* — See the published lectures of Mr. Hilton, of Guy's Hospital.

against which Plato's theories were directed, and the value of the advantages which would be among the results of their realisation.

We must not fail to notice, however, that Plato himself was fully alive to the importance of giving some freedom to the emotions in marriage. For while he assigns to the Rulers the absolute determination of the unions which shall be permitted, he recognises it as one of their most difficult, and at the same time important duties, so to arrange their assignment of men and women to each other, that the decision may appear the result of fortune, not of policy.

*Limits to the regulation of marriage.*

Rep. v. 40.

The offspring of the marriages of the Guardians are to be removed from their mothers as soon as born, that no special attachments may be formed towards those who are all brought forth for the State, and the property of the State in common; and the children of inferior parents, or those which happen to be deformed, are to be made away with,* that the breed may be

*The nurture of children.*

---

\* κατακρύπτειν need not necessarily bear a stronger meaning than that which Curtius assigns to similar expres-

maintained in vigour and purity. Those approved by the authorities are to be transferred to State nurseries, and given over to the nurses who dwell there; the mothers are to be allowed to come and feed them, but the greatest care is to be taken that no mother recognises her own child. In the Laws, where Plato goes much more into detail than he does in the Republic, we find abundant precepts given as to the manner in which the nurses are to rear the children. Just as the Athenian bird-fanciers were accustomed to take long walks in the country, with their cocks and quails tucked under their arms, for the sake of health, "that is to say, not their own health, but the health of the birds;" so the children are to be kept constantly in motion. "They should live, if that were possible, as if they were always rocking at sea." The nurses are to be constantly

---

sions used of the Spartan custom (cp. p. 10). In Timaeus, p. 19 A, where there is an evident reference to this passage, Plato says, "You remember how we said that the children of the good parents were to be brought up (θρεπτέον), and the children of bad parents *secretly dispersed*—εἰς τὴν ἄλλην πόλιν." Cp. Grote's Plato, iii. 205 (note).

carrying them about, and not to allow them to walk until they are three years old, that their legs may not be distorted from the too early use of them. He entirely disapproves of the common custom of scaring children into good behaviour by fearful stories, and insists that only authorised tales should be used by the mothers and nurses. They should be kept as free as possible from every pain and fear, but their pleasures should also be limited, in order that they may be preserved from undue excitement in either direction. Amusements they will be able to provide for themselves abundantly, as they get a little older; all that will be needful is that they should be brought together at the temples of the various villages, in the charge of the nurses, and under the superintendence of one of the twelve women annually appointed for that purpose. With regard to the education which is to be given to them, when they are of the proper age—an age which Plato considers to begin at seven years—he expressly says that it would be difficult to find a better than the

*Laws,* vii. pp. 789–790.

*Rep.* ii. 377.

*Laws,* vii. 792 C–D. *Their amusements.*

*Their education.*

*Rep.* ii. 376. old-fashioned sort, that is, gymnastics for the body and music for the soul. The first three years are to be given up mainly to gymnastics: though the laudatory manner in which he refers to the Egyptian custom of teaching children the principles of arithmetic by means of games (Laws, vii. 819), shows us that he would not have objected to some intermixture of mental training with the physical: but the regular study of letters was not to begin before ten years of age, and only three years were to be assigned to it; at thirteen years a boy was to take in hand the lyre, and at this he might continue for another three years, "neither more nor less: and whether his father or himself liked or disliked the study, he was not to be allowed to spend more or less time in learning music than the law allowed" (Laws, vii. 810). Throughout the whole of his period of pupilage the strictest supervision and discipline were to be exercised. "For neither sheep nor any other animals ought to live without a shepherd, nor ought boys to live without tutors (παιδαγωγοί) any more than slaves

*Strictness of supervision.*

## STRICTNESS OF SUPERVISION. 115

without masters. And of all creatures the boy is the most unmanageable. For, inasmuch as he has in him a spring of reason not yet regulated, he is the most insidious, sharp, and insubordinate of creatures. So that he must be bound with many bridles: in the first place, when he gets away from mothers and nurses, he must be under the control of tutors, because of his childishness and foolishness; and then again as being free-born, he must be kept in check by those who have anything to teach him, and by his studies; but as being, on the other hand, in the position of a slave, any of the free-born citizens may punish him, ay, and his tutor and teacher, if any of them do anything wrong; and he who comes across him and does not inflict upon him the punishment which he deserves, shall incur the greatest disgrace; and that one of the guardians of the laws who has been selected to govern the children, must look after any one who has fallen in with the cases we have mentioned, and has failed to inflict punishment, or has inflicted it improperly: and we must have

Cp. S. Paul, Galat. iv. 1. λέγω δὲ, ἐφ' ὅσον χρόνον ὁ κληρονόμος, νήπιός ἐστιν οὐδὲν διαφέρει δούλου, κύριος πάντων ὤν.

him always looking out sharply and with especial care to the training of the children, directing their natures, and always turning them towards the good, in accordance with the laws." (Laws, vii., 808-9).

*Detailed regulations in the Laws.*

It is characteristic of the dogmatic and despotic tone which marks the Laws throughout that very little freedom of action is given to the national Minister of Education. "As far as possible the law ought to leave nothing to him, but to explain everything, that he may be the interpreter and tutor of others." Hence the multiplicity of details as to the time to be spent in the various studies, the rhythms to be allowed in the poems learnt, and the dances to be practised. In the Republic Plato insists that the same education should be given to boys and girls, that both alike should be trained to be guardians of the State, and that both should practise the exercises of the palaestra. He is aware of the ridicule that such a proposal will bring upon him; but inasmuch as nature has not made man and woman to differ in kind of excellence

*Boys and girls trained alike.*

but only in degree, he will be no partner to any arbitrary distinctions. It is idle to say that gymnastic exercises are not becoming to women: they are needful for the object he has in view; the object is a worthy one, and the best of all maxims that are current or ever will be is that "that which is useful is honourable, and that which is harmful is disgraceful." But in the Laws he is willing to make some concession to what he still regards as the unreasonable prejudices of society, and though he would prefer that boys and girls should be trained together in precisely the same exercises, and with a view to the same functions in after life, he allows them to be educated separately after the age of six years, boys under the care of men, and girls under that of women. But he protests that this is but a second-best kind of polity, better than the Spartan system, and very much better than the Athenian, but after all providing but inadequately for the well-being and happiness of half of the human race. In the Laws we have, as we have noticed

Cp. Rep. v. 457.

Laws, vii. 806-7.

already, many more details as to the method of education than are given in the Republic, where the object is rather to lay down the leading principles which are to govern it. For instance, the following passage comes from the former work, and has nothing corresponding to it in the latter: "The buildings for gymnasia and schools open to all are to be in three places in the midst of the city; and outside the city and in the surrounding country there shall be schools for horse exercise, and open spaces also in three places, arranged with a view to archery and the throwing of missiles, at which young men may learn and practise. In these several schools let there be dwellings for teachers, who shall be brought from foreign parts by pay, and let them teach the frequenters of the school the art of war and the art of music; and they shall come not only if their parents please, but if they do not please; and if their education is neglected, there shall be compulsory education of all and sundry, as the saying is, as far as this is possible;

*Gymnasia and schools.*

*Compulsory education.*

and the pupils shall be regarded as belonging to the State rather than to their parents." (Laws, vii. 804.)

But it is to the Republic especially that we have to look for the principles on which such detailed rules are ultimately based. Plato's theories on education are intimately connected with his psychology and metaphysics. For the moral training of the citizen of his ideal State—a training which is not limited to the period of youth, but extends throughout the whole of life, and which is distinctly viewed as preparatory to another life in which it is to be carried out in fuller perfection—has for its aim the proportionate and harmonious developement of the various elements of the soul; and his intellectual training is intended to fit him for the contemplation of the ideal Good, by the cultivation of the power and habit of abstraction. The soul, according to Plato, is composed of three parts, corresponding generally to the senses, the heart, and the intellect: the first and lowest is the concupiscent principle, or appetite (τὸ ἐπιθυμητικόν); the second

*Principles of education.*

See Jowett's Plato, vol. ii. p. 152.*

*Psychology of Plato.*

the impulsive principle or passion (θυμὸς or τὸ θυμοειδές); the third and highest is reason (τὸ λογιστικόν). The virtue of the first is temperance; the virtue of the second, courage; the virtue of the third is wisdom; while the supreme and crowning virtue, in which the others find their synthesis and harmony, justice, or rather perhaps *rightness*, is only attained to when "the appetites whose object is sensual pleasure, and the impulses that prompt to energetic action," willingly submit to the control of a wisely-ruling reason. The aim of education, then, must be to produce in the appetites temperance, in the spirit courage, in the reason wisdom, and in all that harmonious co-operation which alone is worthy of the name of justice. The earliest instrument employed for the training of children consists of myths or fictitious stories. Here Plato accepts the common practice of his time; but of the majority of the fables used he strongly disapproves. For some of them, he says, tend to corrupt the mind, by placing before it false conceptions of what is to be desired and what is to

*Rep.* iv. 436–441.

Dr. Thompson, Phaedrus, Append. i. p. 166.

*Use of myths.*

*Rep.* ii. 377.

be shunned; while others, and especially those which describe the terrors of Hades, fill it with baseless and degrading fears. The narrative form of composition is especially approved; but if poets adopt the mimetic or dramatic style, they are not to be allowed to assume the characters of vicious or foolish men; no imitation can be suffered but that of the reasonable and virtuous man. In the same way, artists must not venture to present before the eyes of the young copies of any ugly or unbecoming type; their object must be to discover and reproduce the idea of the beautiful; so that children, having before them constantly various forms of beauty, may be fitted to receive and appreciate the influence of beautiful discourse. It is needless to repeat, after what has been said above, that foremost among the creations of art stood music, in its several branches of harmony, rhythm, and lyric verse. The power which these possess to attune the mind unconsciously to the love of the beautiful is dwelt upon at length. The reason why musical training is so

Rep. iii. 396–398. Plato's dislike of the drama comes out again in the Laws, iv. 719 B. Cp. Gorg. 502 B.

Rep. iii. 401.

*Power of music.*

powerful is "because rhythm and harmony find their way into the secret places of the soul, on which they mightily fasten, bearing grace in their movements, and making the soul graceful of him who is rightly educated, or ungraceful if ill-educated; and also because he who has received this true education of the inner being will most shrewdly perceive omissions or faults in art or nature, and with a true taste, while he praises and rejoices over, and receives into his soul the good, and becomes noble and good, he will justly blame and hate the bad, now in the days of his youth, even before he is able to know the reason of the thing: and when reason comes he will recognise and salute her as a friend with whom his education has made him long familiar."

*Rep.* iii. 401-2 (Jowett).

*Platonic Eros.* This love for the beautiful, engendered by a rightly-ordered music, leads Plato on to the general question of the nature and results of that passionate and ecstatic yearning for a closer union with the beautiful, known as the Platonic Eros. To this, as might have been expected from the writer of the Phaedrus and the Symposium, Plato attaches great importance. But just as we have seen already that there is no reason for imputing any taint of evil to the intimacy between the lover and the loved one at Sparta—whatever was the case at Athens—so Plato is careful to preserve his conception of *Eros* free from sensuality and impurity. Then he passes on to the consideration of the gymnastics to be practised. These are intended only in a subordinate degree for the developement of the bodily powers (III. 410 C); just as the main object of music was to infuse temperance, so gymnastics is especially intended to stimulate the spirited (τὸ θυμοειδὲς) part of the nature of man, and thus to increase his courage. The two must be duly tempered, each with the other; lest on the one hand a boy should grow hard and fierce, or on the other his spirit should be melted and softened beyond what is good for him. But Plato does not think it needful to give prescriptions in detail as to gymnastics: "if the mind be properly edu-

*Rep.* iii. 403 B.

cated, the minuter care of the body may be committed to it;" for "the good soul improves the body, and not the good body the soul." And here he leaves the subject of the education of the greater number of the Guardians (in the wider sense in which he employs the term), only providing that at certain stages in their growth there shall be tests imposed upon them. Tasks are to be set before them such that there is a danger of their forgetting their duty or being deceived; toils and pains and conflicts are to be prescribed; and finally, they must be tried by the witcheries of pleasure "more thoroughly than gold is tried in the fire," in order to discover whether they are armed against all enchantments, and of a noble bearing always, good Guardians of themselves and of the music which they have learned, and whether they retain, under all circumstances, a rhythmical and harmonious nature, such as will be most serviceable to the man himself and to the State. And he who at every age, as boy and youth and in mature life, has

*Rep. iii. 403 D.*

*Tests of the Guardians.*

*Rep. iii. 413.*

come out of the trial victorious and pure, shall be appointed a Ruler and Guardian of the State. Those who fail are to be degraded into the class of husbandmen and artisans; but, on the other hand, proved and tested excellence may raise a man from the lower rank to that of Guardian or Auxiliary. Mr. Jowett admirably notices this "career open to talents" as "one of the most remarkable conceptions of the Republic, because un-Greek in character and also unlike anything that existed at all in that age of the world." It is true that Plato says *Plato, ii. 38.* nothing of the means by which the lower class are to attain to the excellence which is so carefully cultivated in the Guardians: throughout the whole of the dialogue they fall into the background: but at least he does not deliberately doom them to entire exclusion from the higher life of the nation.

The subject of the higher training to be afforded to the select Guardians who are to become the Rulers of his ideal State Plato recurs to in the sixth and seventh books *Higher training of Rulers.*

of the Republic. But this does not appear to fall strictly within the scope of the present essay, and may therefore be passed over lightly. The main object which he has in view is to train the chosen few, by the study of philosophy, to the contemplation of the ideal Good. If they have learnt to know what this is, they will be able to recognise it under all the various forms in which it may present itself, and so they will be able to rule aright. "The power which supplies the objects of real knowledge with the truth that is in them, and which gives to him who knows them the power of knowing them, we must consider to be the essential Form and Idea of Good, and we must regard this as the origin of science and of truth, so far as the latter comes within the range of knowledge." The highest of all cognitions of the Form of Good is that of the Dialectician, who comprehends directly the pure essence of Good by means of νοῦς or Intellect (the "Reason" of Kant and Coleridge); an inferior power is that of the Geometer, who knows the Good only through particular

<small>Rep. vi. 505.</small>

<small>Ib. 508 D.</small>

assumptions by means of the διάνοια or the Understanding.  The ordinary life of man is illustrated by the famous simile of captives chained in a gloomy cave, with their backs turned to the opening, so that they can see nothing by the light of the sun, but only the shadows of things cast by a subterranean fire.  The purpose of education is to turn men round from their cramped and confusing position, to enable them to see the glimpses of light which come from the world of brightness and realities, to induce them to struggle up into the light, and to learn to look upon things as they really are, and then to descend again into the cave, that they may benefit those who are still imprisoned, by their fuller and clearer knowledge.  What are the studies then which are needful for education? (τί ἂν οὖν εἴη μάθημα ψυχῆς ὁλκὸν ἀπὸ τοῦ γιγνομένου ἐπὶ τὸ ὄν;) Music and gymnastics are but preparatory studies, both concerned with the changeable and perishing; the useful arts are simply degrading to the reason.  But arithmetic, if taught, not as it is too often with a view to practical

*Ib.* 510–511.

Rep. vii. 514–521.

*Subsidiary studies.*

utility, but as a means of stimulating thought, and as leading us to distrust the impressions of the senses, will be found of value. "The philosopher must study it, because he is bound to rise above the changing and cling to the real, on pain of never becoming a skilful reasoner." The second study is to be geometry, pursued in the same manner and for a like purpose. Geometry of three dimensions, Plato held, was in his time studied absurdly; but if properly taught and honoured, it would suitably take the next place. Treatises on the subject he regards, most justly from his own point of view, as of little value compared with the intellectual discipline furnished by a competent teacher. Astronomy takes the fourth place; but this is to be studied, not by the empiric method of observation, but as a branch of solid geometry, treating of bodies in motion.\* When the philosopher has added to these

---

\* Mr. Jowett notices (Plato, ii. 85) that this view, which at first sight seems so strange, is really supported by the fact that the greater part of astronomy at the present day consists of abstract dynamics, and that the most brilliant discoveries have been made by its means.

the theoretical study of acoustics and harmonics, he will have been trained to see the common method and principle which pervades them all; and so he will be prepared to enter on the crowning task of his life-long work, the pursuit of dialectics. It *Dialectics.* is this which gives his intellect power to grasp the pure and absolute Idea of Good, to rise out of the darkness of the cave, and to gaze upon the eternal realities in the "white-dry" light of truth. The special time allotted to the commencement of these higher studies is the period between thirty and thirty-five years of age; they Rep. vii. 539. should not begin them before this time; for boys, when first introduced to dialectics, are like puppies, who delight in pulling and tearing to pieces with their newly-grown teeth all that comes in their way, merely for amusement's sake. At thirty-five they *Practical duties.* are to be constrained to return to the cave, as it were, and to take upon them the duties of practical life, subjected all the time to the supervision and the continual testing of their seniors, to see if they will remain steadfast in spite of every seduction.

K

It is only when they are fifty years of age, that those who have passed safely through every temptation are to be allowed to resume their philosophical pursuits, and "to lift up the eye of the soul and fix it upon that which gives light to all things." Yet each, when his turn comes, "is to devote himself to the hard duties of public life, and to hold office for his country's sake, not as a desirable, but as an unavoidable occupation; and thus having trained up a constant supply of others like themselves to fill up their place as Guardians of the State, they will depart and take up their abode in the islands of the blessed." The whole of the system of training prescribed for the Guardians is, in accordance with Plato's fundamental position on this point, to be common to men and women. In no respect is any difference to be recognised between them, except such as inevitably result from their natural distinctions.*

Rep. vii. 540.

Cp. Rep. iv. 451-457.

---

\* The earnestness with which Plato aims at raising the education of women from the absolute neglect which it suffered at Athens, is selected both by Jowett and by Zeller (Philosophie, II. 1, 570) as among his greatest excellences.

## ALTERED VIEWS.

The same opinion is maintained in the Laws explicitly. But in other points we find his views largely modified. There is no distinct class of Guardians; their place is filled by a Nocturnal Council,* consisting of the ten oldest "guardians of the laws" and those of the citizens who had obtained prizes for virtue, together with those who had visited foreign countries (a privilege rarely conceded), and an equal number of "co-optative" juniors. This council is asserted to require a special training, but none such is provided for it: the attempt which has been made in the Epinomis (probably by Philippus of Opus: cp. Diog. Laert. iii. 37) to supply the deficiency is certainly not genuine.† But the most important point of all, is that magistrates are to be elected by the votes of all the citizens capable of military service, the

*Laws*, vii. 804-806. *Altered views of the Laws.*

*Laws*, vi. 755.

---

\* It is not easy to see from the text of Plato (Laws, xii. 961 A) how Mr. Jowett arrives at the number of twenty-six for this council.

† Mr. Grote, I believe, stands alone among modern scholars in his attempt to defend it; but his interpretation of the words of Diogenes is to me quite untenable. Mr. Jowett has no doubt upon the subject. Plato, iv. 485 and 172\*. Cp. Zeller, ii. 1. 321.

council by universal suffrage tempered by a division into classes analogous to that prescribed by the Servian constitution at Rome, and even the Minister of Education, the most important functionary in the State, in Plato's view, by the votes of the guardians of the law, who are themselves chosen by the people. The absolute ignoring of the Demus, which is so conspicuous in the Republic, is absent from the Laws, and the education ordained is common to all the citizens. The leading features of this have been already pointed out (pp. 116-119).* We have every-

*Education in the Laws.*

---

\* The most important difference between the teaching of the Republic and that of the Laws as to the higher education lies in the fact that in the Laws there is no mention of the doctrine of Ideas: "the will of God, the standard of the legislator, and the dignity of the soul as compared with the body have taken their place in the mind of Plato." On the other hand, even more importance is attached to the study of Numbers; and this not from the practical utility of a knowledge of arithmetic; this would be by far the most foolish of all arguments (Laws, vii. 818); but because they appertain essentially to the divine nature and to the constitution of the universe. As Zeller justly says: "In this work also Plato could not be content with the common training in music and gymnastics; but the higher training in dialectics he deliberately sets aside; it only remains for him therefore to complete his system with what ought to have been only a preliminary stage to philosophy, a link between mere conception and philosophic thought, that is, the mathematic

where the most rigid censorship, the most precise prescription of duties, and, worse than all in the view of modern thinkers, an elaborate system of perpetual *espionage*. All the regulations are directed to the maintenance of the institutions of the legislator. Plato's noble confidence in the power of reason to guide to the truth (as expressed in passages like Phaedo, 89-91) is exchanged for a timid dread of entrusting a weapon so dangerous to unskilful hands. Originality is in every way discouraged, and the willingness to "follow the argument, whithersoever it might lead," is sacrificed to an oppressive orthodoxy. The ideal of Plato would have been realised in the boast of M. Duruy, as he drew his watch from his pocket: "At this moment

Cp. Grote, Plato, ii. 154–157.

sciences, and to seek in them that complement of the ordinary morality and popular religion, which the original Platonic State had secured by philosophy" (Die Philosophie der Griechen, ii. 1, 621). For the moral side of education much recourse is had to two forces that are but sparingly introduced in the Republic—the religious feeling, and the power of public opinion. It is to the latter that Plato looks to suppress all irregular and harmful sexual relations, just as it has already extinguished incest. The former permeates the whole work, and the entire system of the State is based upon religion. Cp. Zeller, ii. 1, 620.

in every school of France the boys are learning such-and-such a page of such-and-such a text-book." He seems to have forgotten what he once knew—that the wise man is sure to be in opposition to the rest of mankind; for some degree of eccentricity generally accompanies originality; as Democritus said, "the philosopher, if we could see him, would appear to be a strange being." In the Magnesian State all the citizens are to be reduced to rule and measure; there would have been none of those great men "whose acquaintance is beyond all price;" and Plato would have found that in the worst-governed Hellenic State there was more of a *carrière ouverte* for extraordinary genius and virtue than in his own. The first principle of Plato's Laws, borrowed apparently from the Spartan military system, "that no one is to be without a commander," is literally that of the Jesuit order.

Jowett, Plato, iv. 165*.

# CHAPTER IV.

### ARISTOTLE ON EDUCATION.

THE theories of Aristotle upon education bear in many respects a striking resemblance to those of Plato. He is wholly at one with his master in regarding a well-ordered education as the necessary basis of the constitution of a State, and in attaching the greatest importance to the influence of music. Like Plato he regards education, not as pertaining only to the period of youth, but as a life-long task.* And he would place it not less absolutely under the control of the authorities. The supreme good for man, and the ultimate object of all his manifold endeavours, is happiness;

*Place of education in politics.*

---

* This view is often incidentally given in the Politics, but comes out most explicitly in Eth. Nic. x. 10.

and happiness is shown in the Nicomachean Ethics by an exhaustive analysis to be "the conscious activity of the highest part of man according to the law of his own excellence, not unaccompanied by adequate external conditions." The greater part of the Ethics is taken up with the determination of the contents of this "law of excellence" for man. But an important portion of the question is reserved for the Politics. For the law of man's excellence must be ascertained by a complete consideration of his nature (φύσις); and his φύσις plainly shows him to be a political creature (πολιτικὸν ζῷον), much more so than the bee or any other gregarious animal. So that really τῇ φύσει, the State is anterior to the family or to any individual; and therefore individuals are to be regarded primarily and essentially as members of a community. But here, too, comes in that limitation of the idea of a State which we have noticed already in Sparta, in Athens, and in Plato's ideal Republic. In a perfect State all the citizens should be happy; the attainment of his own supreme good by every indi-

Pol. i. 2, 10.

vidual is the very *raison d'être* of a State, and at the same time the necessary condition of its existence. But men can only be happy by virtue, and those who are not capable of the highest excellence have no right to citizenship. Not only slaves but also artisans are excluded by the conditions of their life from attaining to this supreme excellence. Therefore "the best civic community will never admit an artisan (βάναυσον) to the franchise;" or, if such be admitted, the whole conception of the ideal excellence of a citizen must be modified: "for it is not possible to care for the things of virtue while living the life of an artisan or a slave." The citizen is he who is able to take his share in all the duties and honours of civic life; and the purpose of education is to enable him to do so aright.

Pol. iii. 5, 3.

Now that which makes men "political," and raises them above the beasts, is the possession of reason and language.* If, therefore, the supreme good of man is the

*Aristotle's Psychology.*

---

* The meaning of λόγος in the Politics seems to vary between these two ideas, or rather perhaps to comprise them both. Cp. Pol. i. 2, 10, with Pol. vii. (iv.) 15.

conscious activity of his highest part, it is evident that the main aim of education must be the perfect developement of reason: ὁ δὲ λόγος ἡμῖν καὶ ὁ νοῦς τῆς φύσεως τέλος. ὥστε πρὸς τούτους τὴν γένεσιν καὶ τὴν τῶν ἐθῶν δεῖ παρασκευάζειν μελέτην (Pol. iv. (vii.) 15, 8). But although this is the most important object, it does not follow that it is to be the first attended to. In time the lower has to come before the higher, the means before the end. Man consists not only of soul (ψυχή) but also of body; and the soul itself consists of that which is possessed of reason (τὸ λόγον ἔχον), and that which is irrational (τὸ ἄλογον), the latter being divided again into the purely vegetative life, common to man with plants and animals (τὸ θρεπτικὸν or φυτικόν), and that which to a certain extent shares in reason (μετέχον πῃ λόγου), the appetitive and passionate part of the immaterial principle.* The first thing, therefore, to be attended to is the training of the body; the second is the moral educa-

*marginalia:* Cp. the passages quoted by Zeller, ii. 2, 392.

*marginalia:* The order of education.

---

* Eth. Nic. i. 13. In Pol. iv. (vii.) 14, of the last it is said, τὸ δ' οὐκ ἔχει μὲν καθ' αὑτό, λόγῳ δ' ὑπακούειν δυνάμενον.

tion of the desires and passions; the third and highest task is the developement of the reason. But it must be borne in mind throughout that the first two are not ends in themselves, but only means to an end; that the body is trained for the sake of the soul, and the passions for the sake of the intellect. All the citizens are to share the same education, whether they are to be rulers or subjects—and this will be determined by age rather than by anything else —for all the members of the State are to be made as good as possible. But he by no means accepts the doctrine of Plato, insisted upon in the Republic, though reasserted with much less emphasis in the Laws, that the training of men and women is to be identical. On the contrary, he lays much stress on their essential differences, and maintains that their virtues are far from identical. While the slave has no will at all, and the child's is immature, the woman's is invalid (ἄκυρον), and waits for the sanction of her lord (κύριος). So in the case of moral excellences, we must admit that all possess them, but they vary not

*Education common to all.*

Pol. iv. (vii.) 14.

*The differences between men and women.*

Pol. i. 13, 7–11.

only in degree but also in kind. The man's virtues are those of rule, the woman's those of obedience; hence self-control, courage, and justice will be different in her case from what they are in his. Men have been misled by the use of vague generalities; but the real state of the case is clear as soon as we examine the matter in detail; for instance:

Soph. Aj. 261.   A modest silence well becomes a woman,

but this is far otherwise with a man. Therefore their whole system of training must be different, and it will require a separate consideration. But this he nowhere bestows upon it, and therefore we are not in possession of his views on this important branch of the subject. We have some clue to the manner in which he would probably have handled it in the following passage from the Hist. Anim. ix. 1. (p. 608 B, ed. Bekker: Berl.). "Females are tenderer and more mischievous and less straightforward, more hasty, and more given to thought for the nourishment of their offspring; but males, on the other hand, are more spirited, fiercer, more

Pol. i. 13, 15.
Cp. Zeller, ii. 534 (note 2), and St. Hilaire, *ad loc*.

## THE NATURE OF WOMAN. 141

straightforward and less treacherous. A woman exceeds a man in pitifulness and in her tendency to tears, but on the other hand she is more given to envy and censoriousness, to abusiveness and blows. Again, the female is more inclined than the male to be dispirited and despondent; she is more shameless and more false, and at the same time more easily deceived, and of a better memory; she is also more wakeful, but more sluggish, and generally less disposed to move than man, and she needs less food. The male, as we have said, is more ready to give help, and more courageous than the female." We may hesitate before we call this, with Zeller (ii. 2. 535, note 1), "a careful observation of natural history," especially as traits drawn from Laconian bitches, bears, and female cuttle-fishes are without hesitation transferred to women. But it is a sufficient proof that Aristotle would have treated the question of their education in a very different way from that which Plato adopted upon a hasty generalisation as to their absolute identity of nature with men. In the imperfect discussion of the subject of education contained in the Politics, it is boys and youths who are in view throughout.

As has been said before, the ultimate aim of all the State-education of the citizens is the full developement of the intellectual powers. But reason (λόγος) admits of division; there is practical reason, concerned with the affairs of daily life, and contemplative reason (ὁ θεωρητικός). Which of these is it that has the strongest claims upon our attention? Aristotle, who in the Nicomachean Ethics has determined the supreme happiness for man to reside in the greatest possible continuity of intellectual exercise, can have no doubt how he is to answer. As war is to be pursued only for the sake of peace, and business only for the sake of leisure, so the functions of the practical reason are of value only as needful for fuller and more perfect exercise of the speculative reason. This has been too much lost sight of by legislators, who have regarded success in war as a thing to be sought for its own sake; and conse-

*The life of action and the life of contemplation.*

quently their States have been in a healthy condition so long as they have been engaged in war; but they have been ruined by peace, losing the temper (βαφή) of their spirit, because they have never been educated to a proper use of leisure. In Aristotle's time the decay of Sparta furnished a striking proof of the inadequacy of a merely military training for the life of a nation; and he does not fail to make use of it to point his moral. Therefore, the object of the legislator must be to inspire those virtues which are best adapted to secure a wise and happy enjoyment of peace and leisure. Courage and endurance are mainly needed for times of active duty; temperance and justice are also required then, but still more in leisure and tranquillity, while philosophy is especially appropriate to the latter condition. To produce these virtues we need the co-operation of (1) the natural disposition, (2) habits that become instinctive, and (3) a right reason. The last is most important, but it is the last to appear in the life of a child; its habits precede its

Pol. iv. (vii.) 15, 10.

reasoning judgments, and the habits are themselves preceded by natural tendencies. Therefore, as we saw before, the care of the body is the first thing, then the care of the passions, and finally the discipline of the intellect.

*Pol. iv. (vii.) 1–2, 1422.*

*Regulation of marriage.*

With Aristotle, as with Plato, the legislator's care for the physical well-being of the citizens commences with the regulation of marriage. The special points to be provided against are a disparity of age between husband and wife, and too early marriages, which have the double disadvantage that the offspring is likely to be puny, and that they are too near the age of the father, and so not likely to reverence him as they should. The proper age for marriage is pronounced to be eighteen for women and thirty-seven for men; the main reason for such a wide interval between the two is apparently that the procreative power in husband and wife may cease at about the same time. Detailed regulations follow as to the physical conditions needful for securing healthy offspring. Infants who are born deformed are not to be reared,

*Rearing of infants.*

## REARING OF CHILDREN.

and if the population appears to be pressing on the limits fixed by the constitution, abortion is to be practised in the early stages of the growth of the embryo.* Much stress is laid upon the quality of the food given to children when young, and Aristotle appears to approve of the mechanical appliances used, as he says, by some nations to straighten their limbs. Until they are five years of age they are not to be set to any studies, nor to any compulsory work, but activity of body is to be promoted by proper amusements, and their frames are to be hardened by exposure to cold. Differing here from the Spartan legislator [see p. 20] Aristotle will not have them forbidden to cry;† συμφέρει γὰρ πρὸς αὔξησιν;

---

\* This precept of Aristotle's did not find universal acceptation even in Greece. Cp. Stobaeus, 74, 61, and 75, 15 (quoted by Schömann Alterth. i. 112, note). But in Rome there is no trace of any law against *abortio partus* before A.D. 200. Cicero (pro Cluent. 11, 32) has to go to Miletus for an example of its punishment. Cp. Daremberg and Saglio: Dict. Ant. p. 16.

† Congreve, on Pol. iv. (vii.) 17, 6, apparently takes διατάσεις to refer to physical exertions generally; but it must surely be here limited to "shouts." Cp. the use of ἐντεινάμενος in Plat. Rep. 536 C; Ar. Nub. 968, "les cris et les pleurs," St. Hilaire.

it acts as a gymnastic exercise for little children. Like Plato he holds that the stories which they are told should be only such as are sanctioned by the authorities; they are to be kept away, as far as possible, from the society of slaves, and are not to be allowed to witness any of the buffooneries which the laws allow in the worship of some of the gods. Aristotle is indeed somewhat doubtful whether any such exhibitions are to be suffered at all; but he reserves this point for a more detailed examination, which is not found in his extant works. The point on which he lays especial stress is that the *first* impressions left upon the mind of a child should be wholly free from every kind of evil:—ὥσπερ γὰρ φασὶ τὰ κενὰ τῶν ἀγγείων ἀναφέρειν τὰς τῶν πρώτων εἰς αὐτὰ ἐγχυθέντων ὀσμάς, οὕτω καὶ αἱ τῶν νέων ψυχαί. From the age of five to that of seven children are to be lookers-on at the lessons, which afterwards they will have to learn; and then they are to be taken under the more immediate supervision of the State.

But now that he has come to the

<small>See St. Hilaire, Politique d'Aristote, p. 260.</small>

<small>Philo, quoted by Orelli on Hor. Ep. 1, 2, 69.</small>

threshold of education proper, Aristotle raises three questions: (1.) Ought there to be any public authoritative system of education? (2.) Ought it to be the same for all? (3.) If so, in what should it consist? The first two are easily answered from his point of view; indeed the theories upon which he has been building up the whole of his ideal of a State, will only allow them to be answered in one way. For in the Nicomachean Ethics (ii. 1.) he has shown that a previous training from childhood up is needful for virtuous actions (inasmuch as virtue resides not in the act, but in the moral state (ἕξις) from which it springs); and in the tenth book of the same work (c. 10) he has shown that the previous training can only, or at any rate can best, be had through a system based upon public authority. And this is not only the case in the ideal State: it is even more true in imperfect States like the democratic or the oligarchic: for every constitution requires for its stability that the characters of the citizens should be in harmony with it, and this can only be

*Nature of the State education.*

secured by a State-ordered system of education. That it must be one and the same for all is proved by a consideration of the fact that the State as a whole can have but one ultimate aim; things of public concern must be dealt with by the public; and it is a grave mistake to suppose that any citizen belongs to himself: far rather does he belong to the State of which he is a member; and the State must determine his education as it sees to be best, without making any distinctions between one and another. But with regard to the things to be taught there is great difference of opinion. Is education to be merely utilitarian, or is it to include moral training, or are the higher refinements* of intellectual culture also to be aimed at? All these views have found supporters; so that the systems actually in vogue help us little. It is certain, however, that useful knowledge ought to form a part of education; but then only that portion of useful know-

<small>Pol. v. (viii.) 1, 2.</small>

---

* τὰ πέριττα seems to be used here much in the same sense as in Aristotle's well-known description of the dialogues of Plato (Pol. ii. 6, 5) with perhaps a touch of depreciation, but hardly as St. Hilaire, "*des objets de pur agrément.*"

ledge is to be sanctioned which is free from all taint of servility. Every art and every study is to be considered servile which renders the body or the soul or the intellect of a freeman unserviceable for the acts and practices of virtue. And under this head come all occupations which are pursued for wages, for they deprive the intellect of leisure and make it abject. Even liberal studies, if pursued too far, or for improper motives, are liable to certain dangers. Perhaps an examination of the various constituents of education in detail may lead us to more general views. These are four in number, for to letters, gymnastics, and music some now add drawing. It is evident that letters and drawing are useful studies; and the same may be said of gymnastics, for this developes that courage and bodily vigour which are needful for the well-being of the State. But what of music? It cannot be said to be useful in the same way as these other pursuits. The ancients always studied it as affording an honourable occupation for leisure, and this is the true view. For the

*Detailed examination of the subjects of education.*

right employment of leisure is one of the most important tasks that can be set to a man. Work is always done for some end, and therefore has not an independent value of its own; but leisure is an end in itself, and can be used at our discretion for the highest purposes. It must not be used for amusement merely, for that would be to make amusement—which is properly only a relief from work—the chief end of life. The main aim of education is to teach a man the right use of leisure; and music has always been justly regarded as one of the noblest and most elevating employments for such time. It may therefore claim its place as one of the most important elements of the higher education. But even those arts which are of direct utility, like reading, writing, and drawing, are not to be learnt solely on the ground of their utility: they may have, if properly taught, a helpful influence on the mind. To resume, then, the detailed consideration of the various branches of education, in order previously decided on:—First, the body is to be trained by the gymnast and the

*Gymnastics.*

"paedotribe." But care is to be taken that gymnastics do not pass into athletics (cp. p. 28), and that they are not carried so far as to injure the character. The Lacedaemonians, though they have avoided the former error, have fallen into the latter. They have formed their system with a view to courage alone; but, in the first place, no one virtue is to be pursued to the neglect of others; secondly, if any one ought to be so pursued, it certainly is not courage; and thirdly, courage is a very different thing from ferocity, as we may see in the case of many barbarous tribes. Great care must be taken not to overtrain boys in gymnastics, or more evil than good will be the result. Indeed, they must be allowed to spend at least three years in their other studies before they begin any severe gymnastic exercises; for "it is not proper to put the body and the mind to hard work at the same time." We may pause for a moment in this *resumé* of Aristotle's theories to notice how he agrees with Plato on a point which is very strange to our modern ideas. "He seems to have

Pol. v. (viii.) 4, 9.

thought that two things of an opposite and different nature could not be learnt at the same time. We can hardly agree with him, judging by experience of the effect on the mind of spending three years, be-tween the ages of fourteen and seventeen, in mere bodily exercise."

*Jowett, Plato, ii. 154.*

*Music.* Music in its narrower sense was so firmly established in the time of Aristotle as an essential portion of education, that we could have well understood his motives, if he had been content to accept the traditional ideas upon the subject. But, according to his custom, he enters upon a careful analysis of the purposes which music is intended to serve. Is it simply a sensuous gratification, as some assume? Or, has it an ennobling effect upon the character? Or, does it even contribute to the developement of the intellect (φρόνησις), by supplying it with needful relaxation? It is evident that it cannot be simply amusement, or it would form no part of education; for the end of education is not amusement. Nor can it be the case that the boy is trained to music that he may have amusement when he is grown up; for this could be better supplied by the services of professional musicians. Nor can it be pursued only for its effect on the character. In that case, too, there would be no need to learn it personally; and it is recognised that there is something servile (βάναυσον) in a professional study of music. Aristotle's own opinion is, that music may be considered at once a means of education (παιδεία), an amusement (παιδιά), and a source of enjoyment in life (διαγωγή),*—" an ornament of life in its highest form, when the man has passed the restlessness of childhood, ever in want of amusement; has passed the struggles of youth and earlier manhood, the period of learning, of discipline, of formation of character; and has reached the settled state of life and mature manhood, to be spent not in business or in war, but as a period of rest and peaceful

---

* The distinction between παιδιά and διαγωγή appears to be that the former is rather "childish games," the latter "rational relaxation" [cp. v. 5, 10, and Congreve on v. 3, 6]. Liddell and Scott appear to be somewhat misleading. See Zeller, ii. 2, 577, 5.

*Congreve, Politics of Aristotle, p. 220.*

contemplation." It is admitted on all hands to be one of the greatest of pleasures; and that it influences the character is clear from its evident power over the emotions, for it is the emotions which form the character. And as right education consists in training men to feel pleasure at right objects (cp. Nic. Eth. book ii.), the power which music has in this respect must be of the greatest value. The different "modes" are found by experience to have different effects. Mixolydian is plaintive, the Dorian produces a steady calm, the Phrygian excites the passions; and these facts are to be remembered in using them for purposes of education.

*Practical knowledge of music.*

But is it necessary for boys to acquire any skill in performing themselves? Yes: for, in the first place, this will intensify the effect of music upon them; and, secondly, they must have something to do with their hands, or they will be always breaking things. But this practical acquaintance with music is not to be carried so far as to interfere with other studies, or to teach them to perform the wonderful new-fangled flourishes (τὰ θαυμάσια καὶ περιττὰ τῶν ἔργων) which were coming into fashion in Aristotle's time. The flute was to be rejected, as an immoral instrument, unduly exciting, and contributing nothing to real education (Pol. v. 7, 14). Then he proceeds to discuss the rhythms to be permitted: the moral modes alone are to be employed for study, though the more animated and passionate ones may be allowed in concerts, where the audience only listen, without taking any part themselves. A decided preference is expressed for the Dorian mode, and Plato is censured for having in his Republic allowed the Phrygian alone to remain by the side of the Dorian at the same time that he proscribed the music of the flute, which is particularly appropriate to it. A greater variety should be admitted, in view of the different purposes to which music is applied. Only three requisites are always to be kept in mind—the absence of excess (τὸ μέσον), the limits of what is practicable (τὸ δυνατόν), and propriety (τὸ πρέπον).

Cp. Hermann ad Soph. Trach. 216, and the Scholiast there (p. 157, ed. Elmsl.), and Cic. pro Mur. § 29.

Here Aristotle breaks off his formal

discussion of education. Whether the fifth book of the Politics is fragmentary, as Schneider, Stahr, Congreve, and Zeller maintain, or whether it is perfect, as St. Hilaire contends, we cannot decide with certainty. But the weight of authority and of probability appear to incline to the former belief. At all events, we are left to gather the views of Aristotle on the proper training of the intellect of a nation, as best we may, from the principles that are established, and the hints that are dropped in his other treatises. The philosopher who made the supreme good of man to reside in the vigorous and unimpeded play of the intellect, and who, perhaps more than any other of his time, recognised the absolute necessity of a careful and long-continued training to produce this, either never lived to give to the world his matured thoughts on the methods and instruments of this training, or he wrote them down only to share the fate of others of his most precious works. The same caprice of fortune which has preserved to us the treatise "De Gene-

*Incompleteness of the discussion.*

See the very complete discussion of the question in Zeller, ii. 2, 520–527.

ratione Animalium," and robbed us of Πολιτεῖαι, has, it is to be feared, deprived us of what would have been an invaluable criticism on the educational uses of literature, and the means of developing the higher intellectual powers. And even in the case of his Poetics, from which we might have expected to draw some matter for our present purpose, we find on the one hand much that is undoubtedly spurious intermixed, and on the other hand we have a singular incompleteness of treatment, which leaves some of the most important aspects of his subject wholly untouched. It can only be considered as a fragmentary and largely interpolated collection of isolated extracts from Aristotle's original work. The general ends to which he would have directed his training may be gathered to some extent from the Sixth Book of the [Nicomachean] Ethics, where he treats of the intellectual virtues. But here again we must notice, first, that the Aristotelian authorship of this book is more than doubtful. Sir A. Grant has shown, I think almost to demonstration,

Zeller, ii. 2, 75, "die unersetzlichen Politeien."

Zeller, ii. 2, 77, note.

*Aristotle's Ethics, vol. i. pp. 33-43.*

that, with the book which precedes it and that which follows it, it is the work of Eudemus, and that, although on the whole it gives a fair representation of the master's views, it is in some points at variance with them, and on many points obscure. And secondly, the intellectual excellences are regarded not so much in and for themselves, as in relation to their influence in determining the moral canon. Virtue

*Eudemus on the intellectual virtues.*

having been previously defined to be a mean between two extremes, which mean is to be fixed by "right reason," it follows to explain what this "right reason" (ὁ ὀρθὸς λόγος) is. The rational part of the soul is shown to consist of two parts—the one, which may be called the scientific reason (τὸ ἐπιστημονικόν), dealing with necessary principles and the existences depending on them (τὰ τοιαῦτα τῶν ὄντων ὅσων αἱ ἀρχαὶ μὴ ἐνδέχονται ἄλλως ἔχειν); and the other, the calculative reason (τὸ λογιστικόν), to which appertains contingent matter. We have seen before that there are three principles in man—sensation (αἴσθησις), reason (νοῦς), and desire (ὄρεξις)—corresponding to the three parts of his nature. Action results from the synthesis of desire and the practical or calculative reason, when that which is affirmed or desired by the latter is pursued or avoided by the former. Then again it is shown that truth, of whatever kind, is attained only by five organs of the mind (οἷς ἀληθεύει ἡ ψυχή). These are art (τέχνη), science (ἐπιστήμη), wisdom (φρόνησις), philosophy (σοφία), reason (νοῦς): the first is the acquisition of truth, *with a view to production;* the second covers the results of *syllogistic reasoning;* the third is right knowledge, *with a view to action;* the fifth is the organ or mode whereby we arrive at *principles;* and the fourth is higher than all the others, and comprehends both wisdom and reason, the knowledge of particulars and the grasp of principles. The three great divisions of human science—θεολογική, μαθηματική, and φυσική—are but branches of this all-embracing σοφία. In this classification it is evident that the various sections are not co-ordinate; and it seems very possible that Eudemus comprehended but imperfectly, or else has unwisely attempted to improve upon, the psychology of his teacher.* Be this as it may, he has left us without the means of learning by what methods either Aristotle or he would have promoted the developement of these several intellectual excellences, and which of them he would have especially cultivated in a system of national education. We can only say that he would have laid the greatest stress on the formation of virtuous habits, as a means of attaining practical wisdom, οὐ γὰρ οἷόν τε εἶναι ἀγαθὸν κυρίως ἄνευ φρονήσεως οὐδὲ φρόνιμον ἄνευ τῆς ἠθικῆς ἀρετῆς. But this simply brings us back to our former position, that Aristotle attached the greatest importance to an authoritative public discipline of the manners and the intellect, and makes us regret the more deeply that we can form such imperfect conceptions of the detailed form which he would have given to it. That he would have expanded the common curriculum,

*Indication of Aristotle's views.*

---

\* The division given in the Posterior Analytics is much more clear and satisfactory: there we have three pairs mutually contrasted: διάνοια νοῦς, ἐπιστήμη τέχνη, φρόνησις σοφία. Cp. Sir A. Grant on Eth. vi. 4, 1.

at least for the most advanced students, by the addition of a far more scientifie rhetoric, and an all but wholly new logic, by a wide acquaintance with natural science, and a universal application of the historical method of research, may be argued fairly from the contents of his published works; but what in his opinion should be the order of their study, and what the extent to which they should be pursued by various classes of the community, must always remain uncertain. It is only clear, from the well-known expression that young men ought not to study philosophy, that Aristotle would have had a careful and protracted intellectual discipline precede any attempt to grapple with the problems of ethics. To art he would certainly have assigned a larger place in education than Plato did; for while the latter, in his Laws, banishes poets from his ideal State, with but few exceptions; and directs that the youths, instead of committing to memory the epics of Homer or the lays of Simonides, the lofty lines of Æschylus or the melodious choruses of Sophocles, should learn by heart the laws and ordinances of the legislator,* Aristotle accepts with approval not only the tragic, but even the comic drama. Provided that wit does not degenerate into scurrility, and that the dramatist chooses for his attack faults that are really ridiculous, and not serious moral offences—τὸ γὰρ γελοῖόν ἐστιν ἁμάρτημά τι καὶ αἶσχος ἀνώδυνον καὶ οὐ φθαρτικόν—he is willing to recognise its value. His conception of the importance of tragedy in moral education comes out in the much-discussed expression, "effecting a purification of passions such as these by means of pity and fear," δι' ἐλέου καὶ φόβου περαίνουσα τὴν τῶν τοιούτων παθημάτων κάθαρσιν. What the precise meaning of the phrase is, it is far from easy to determine: perhaps the most satisfactory view is that of Zeller, who regards the "purification" as consisting, not in the improvement of the will, or the strengthening of virtuous tendencies, but in the removal of the evils caused

Laws, vii. 811 E; cp. 817 C.

Zeller, ii. 2, 622, 5.

---

* On Plato's views of art, and the dangers to which it is exposed, see Zeller, ii. 1, 613.

by too violent emotions, and in the calming of the passions. This tragedy effects by referring the individual instances of suffering and calamity to the common law of destiny, and by pointing out under all the eternal law of righteousness.

<small>Cp. Zeller, ii. 2, 611–617.</small>

But it is impossible to weave into any consistent and harmonious scheme fragmentary facts like these; and we are obliged to leave imperfect the attempted sketch of the thoughts of "the master of those who know," on what he would himself have regarded as the fundamental question of national education.

A few words may be added in conclusion on some general aspects of the question under our consideration. They have, it is hoped, not been wholly lost sight of in the study of the details; but it may be that they will be brought into a clearer light, when gathered up together by way of a retrospect. There is one point of view from which the national education of Greece appears to us singularly attractive. Like the works of the artists and poets who were trained by it, it possesses

<small>*General aspects of Greek education.*</small>

a unity and completeness within its limits that are all but perfect.* Just as

"The singer of sweet Colonos, and its child,"

who always rises to our thoughts as the crown and flower of the Hellenic genius,

"Saw life steadily, and saw it whole;"

so the Greek education laid its hands on the entire citizen, and, within the range that it recognised, moulded all his powers into a finished unity. Beauty of form, and grace of movement, subtleness of intellect, and nobleness of life were all attained, at least to such an extent as to leave no jarring sense of flagrant discord between the ideal aimed at and the work achieved. This it is that lends so much of the charm of those "self-sufficing" days, in the eyes of those who are wearied and distracted with the manifold claims of the varied developements of modern thought. There is a certain sense of adequacy, of attainment, of perfection, which wins ineffably on those who are harassed with the "blank misgivings," the un-

---

* Cp. the remarks on the ἄσπετος αἰθήρ of Greek literature in the "Guesses at Truth," pp. 39 and 64 (last ed.)

satisfied yearnings, the baffled aspirations, the unsolved problems, that vex alike the life and the literature of our times. And yet we are bound, while we feel very keenly the charm, to recognise the cost at which it was won, a 'cost that we could not and would not pay. The deep dull hue of much of our modern thought is due not solely to the turbid source from which it springs: it comes at least as much from the profundity of the abysses over which it is brooding. If the course of the modern student is often perplexing, it is not because he is called to traverse a desert way, but rather that on every side there branch out by-paths, tempting him away from the road he has chosen by the beauty of the prospects that they offer, or the richness of the fruits that lie on every hand. If the Greeks were not tried by a "Conflict of Studies," such as that in which we find ourselves, it was from the limitation, we may almost dare to add, the poverty, of their intellectual food. It may indeed be that we are now constrained to a specialization

*Contrast of modern thought.*

which leads to a more one-sided and incomplete developement of the whole being of a man than the music and gymnastics of a young Athenian. But if it be found to be so irremediably, we can but take refuge in the faith that none have taught more unwaveringly than the philosophers of Athens, that the well-being of the State brings with it the well-being of all and every one. If "the individual withers," yet "the world is more and more."

*Wider extent of modern education.*
But again, if we ought to be willing to sacrifice something of the perfect and harmonious unity of the Greek education for the sake of a deeper culture, much more should we be content to do this when it is a question of its greater width and extension. As we have already seen, the very phrase of national education in Greece is all but a misnomer. Thanks to the lessons we have learnt from the Gospel of Christ, we cannot look with complacence upon any "national education," however well-rounded and self-sufficing, whose benefits are not shared by the artisan, the peasant and the factory-

hand. The task which the legislators of to-day have set before them is one far harder than any with which Plato or Aristotle dared to grapple. It is to see that every child of Britain's thirty millions has placed within his reach that training which shall fit him most completely to serve his fellow-men in the station in which it has pleased his God to place him. It may be that still we are far from the goal. Educational theorists are debating; class-interests bar the way; and, worst of all, sectarian jealousies wrangle, till it seems at times that the day for which every Christian is longing would never come to us. But come it must at last: and then we shall see in the national schools of England a physical training not inferior to that of Athens or Lacedaemon; heart and soul shall learn to love yet nobler truths than those which dawned before the eyes of Plato; and the wisdom of Aristotle shall be as childish fancies to—

"The fairy-tales of science, and the long results of time."

# BY THE SAME AUTHOR.

*Second Edition. Crown 8vo., price 3s. 6d., cloth.*

**The Light of the World:** an Essay on the Distinctive Features of Christian as compared with Pagan Ethics.

### CRITICAL NOTICES.

"It would be difficult to praise too highly the spirit, the burden, the conclusions, or the scholarly finish of this beautiful essay. There are abundant signs of ripe scholarship, rich culture, and the modesty of extensive knowledge. We accept the volume with singular satisfaction, as a very valuable contribution to Christian Ethics."—*British Quarterly Review.*

"We are not late in paying our tribute to this little volume; it might seem so, from the announcement of the second edition, but in fact the essay has rapidly become popular, and placed itself beyond the necessity of any introduction on our part. It deserves its success. Mr. Wilkins has not only produced the Hulsean Dissertation of the year: he has also written the best essay we have upon his subject. . . . The essay is beautifully written, abounds with the mosaic work of apt quotation from an unusual breadth of reading, and is as remarkable for reverence as for pure taste in other respects."—*London Quarterly Review.*

"A clever and very readable essay. The range, at once, of reading and thought which it exhibits is very striking."—*Literary Churchman.*

"It is not surprising that this most scholarly treatise should have gained the Hulsean Prize, or that it should have rapidly passed into a second edition. It cannot fail to be read with the greatest interest by all students."—*Watchman.*

LONDON: MACMILLAN & CO.

*Crown 8vo., price 5s., cloth.*

**Phœnicia and Israel:** an Historical Essay.

"A thoughtful, learned, and eloquent essay."—*British Quarterly Review.*

"Mr. Wilkins's essay obtained the Burney Prize in the University of Cambridge for the year 1870, and must be reckoned as one of the very best of the many excellent productions which have been called forth by this and kindred distinctions at the two Universities. As an introduction to the study of the subject, his essay is admirable."—*Spectator.*

"The great value of the essay consists in its bringing before the English public, in an easily accessible and attractive form, much information which previously was to be found only in learned works, almost, if not altogether, unknown to the general reader. And this information is very important and interesting, both in quantity and in kind."—*Guardian.*

"As an introduction to the study of Old Testament history, the value of this little book can hardly be exaggerated, not merely for its clearness and vigour of style, but for the variety and abundance of the information it conveys, and the signs which every page shows of careful research and sound critical skill."—*Standard.*

LONDON: HODDER & STOUGHTON.

*Fp. 8vo., price 3s. 6d., cloth.*

## The Orations of Cicero against Catilina,
with Notes and an Introduction. Translated from the German of Karl Halm, with many additions, by A. S. WILKINS, M.A.

"The best school-book, we think, that has ever come under our notice. The excellence of the original is sufficiently guaranteed by its appearing in Haupt and Sauppe's series, and its practical usefulness fully established by the sale of seven editions in the course of a few years. But we do not hesitate to affirm that the English edition is rendered far superior to the original by the extensive additions of Professor Wilkins, which bear ample testimony, not simply to his varied critical and literary acquirements, but also to the correctness of his judgment respecting the difficulties and wants of the generality of students. There is scarcely a note in the original to which important additions have not been made by the editor."—*British Quarterly Review.*

"This very handy little edition of the Catiline Orations is based on the German edition of Halm, to which Mr. Wilkins has added a good many notes of his own, all useful. Most of these additional notes bear on philology; many, however, explain Roman customs and phrases, and there are also frequent parallel examples of Ciceronian usages which are especially useful to a student beginning to make acquaintance with the author. Indeed, we have never seen a book which we should feel more inclined to put into the hands of a boy as a first introduction to the great orator."—*Athenæum.*

LONDON: MACMILLAN & CO.

---

*In the Press. Two vols. 8vo.*

## The Principles of Greek Etymology.
By Professor GEORGE CURTIUS, of the University of Leipzig. Translated by AUGUSTUS S. WILKINS, M.A., Professor of Latin and Comparative Philology in the Owens College, Manchester, and EDWIN B. ENGLAND, M.A., Assistant Lecturer in Classics in the Owens College.

LONDON: JOHN MURRAY.

# NEW BOOKS.

**The Autobiography and Memoir of Thomas Guthrie, D.D.** Edited by his Sons, Rev. David K. Guthrie and Charles J. Guthrie, M.A. 2 vols., post 8vo.

**The Huguenots in France, after** the Revocation of the Edict of Nantes. With a Visit to the Country of the Vaudois. By Samuel Smiles, Author of "The Huguenots: Their Settlements and Industries in England and Ireland," "Self-Help," &c. Crown 8vo.

**The Great Ice Age, and its Relation to the Antiquity of Man.** By James Geikie, F.R.S.E., F.G.S., &c., of H.M. Geological Survey. With numerous Illustrations and Diagrams. Demy 8vo.

**National Education and Public** Elementary Schools. By J. H. Rigg, D.D. Crown 8vo, 12s.

**White Rose and Red: a Love** Story. By the Author of "Saint Abe." Crown 8vo, 6s.

**Memorials of a Quiet Life.** By Augustus J. C. Hare. With 2 Steel Portraits. Ninth Edition. 2 vols. crown 8vo, 21s.

**Holiday Letters.** By M. Betham-Edwards, Author of "A Winter with the Swallows." Crown 8vo, 7s. 6d.

**Revelation Considered as Light:** a Series of Discourses. By the late Right Rev. Alexander Ewing, D.C.L., Bishop of Argyll and the Isles. Post 8vo, 7s. 6d.

## Animals and their Masters.
By the Author of "Friends in Council." Third Edition. Crown 8vo, 7s. 6d.

## Searching the Net: a Book of
Verses. By JOHN LEICESTER WARREN, Author of "Philoctetes." Crown 8vo, 6s.

## The Character of St. Paul.
By J. S. HOWSON, D.D., Dean of Chester. Crown 8vo, 5s.

## The Tragedies of Æschylos.
A New Translation, with a Biographical Essay and an Appendix of Rhymed Choruses. By E. H. PLUMPTRE, M.A., Professor of Divinity in King's College, London. Crown 8vo, 7s. 6d.

## Heroes of Hebrew History.
By SAMUEL WILBERFORCE, D.D., the late Bishop of Winchester. Crown 8vo, 5s.

## Lays of the Highlands and
Islands. By JOHN STUART BLACKIE, Professor of Greek in the University of Edinburgh. Second Edition. Small 8vo, 6s.

## Religious Thought in England,
from the Reformation to the End of Last Century. By the Rev. JOHN HUNT, Author of "An Essay on Pantheism." Complete in 3 vols. demy 8vo, 21s. each.

## Town Geology.
By the Rev. Canon KINGSLEY. Fourth Thousand. Crown 8vo, 5s.

## Lars: a Pastoral of Norway,
By BAYARD TAYLOR. Small 8vo, 3s. 6d.

---

STRAHAN & CO., 56 LUDGATE HILL, LONDON.

www.ingramcontent.com/pod-product-compliance
Lightning Source LLC
Chambersburg PA
CBHW030434190426
43202CB00036B/246